PHILOSOPHY

OF

SKEPTICISM AND ULTRAISM,

WHEREIN

THE OPINIONS OF REV. THEODORE PARKER, AND OTHER WRITERS ARE SHOWN TO BE INCONSISTENT WITH SOUND REASON AND THE CHRISTIAN RELIGION.

BY JAMES B. WALKER,

AUTHOR OF "THE PHILOSOPHY OF THE PLAN OF SALVATION," "GOD REVEALED IN THE PROCESS OF CREATION AND BY THE MANIFESTATION OF CHRIST," ETC.

NEW YORK:
DERBY & JACKSON, 119 NASSAU STREET.
CINCINNATI: RICKEY, MALLORY & WEBB.
CHICAGO: D. B. COOKE & CO.

1857.

STEREOTYPED BY
THOMAS B. SMITH,
82 & 84 Beekman-st.

PRINTED BY
GEO. RUSSELL & CO.,
61 Beekman-st.

TO

Prof. Stowe, Theodore Parker, Joseph Barker;

AND TO ALL THINKERS,

WHETHER THEY BE

CHRISTIAN, SCEPTIC, OR REPROBATE,

This Volume

IS MOST RESPECTFULLY DEDICATED

BY THE AUTHOR.

CONTENTS.

LETTER VIII.

LETTER IX.

LETTER X.

LETTER XI.

LETTER XII.

LETTER XIII.

LETTER XIV.

PREFACE.

IN the following pages the author has endeavored to meet, in a popular form, some of the prevailing moral fallacies of the times.

It is admitted by every one who has observed the state of public opinion in relation to moral and religious questions, that no inconsiderable portion of the business men of our cities and villages—especially the young men—are influenced by opinions which are inconsistent both with sound reason and with revelation. This little volume is an endeavor to bring back some who have wandered, to a rational apprehension of religious doctrine and duty.

It asks the forbearance of the dogmatic theologian. The effort of the author is to give the *rationale* of the Christian doctrines which he discusses. Those for whom these letters are mostly designed have chosen reason, rather than revelation, as arbiter in matters of faith. We have, therefore, permitted reason to speak *freely* in behalf of revealed truth, and to speak sometimes in forms of language that we would not use with those who are believers in divine revelation.

We have, in the discussion, waived all questions not involved in the main issues, and have granted to the opposers and accusers of the evangelical ministry all that a fair mind can ask; and as the skeptics of our day claim a philosophical basis for many of their opinions, we have endeavored to meet them on their own ground.

One of the volumes of Rev. Theodore Parker (Discourses of Religion) was put into our hands by a friend. We read it, and were surprised to find a book strong in phrase and assuming in rhetoric; but without congruity, and, as it seemed to us, out of harmony both with reason and revelation.

With this view of the book, we commenced a series of letters to a friend, one of which was published in a religious journal. Other letters were written, but not published. In those letters we referred, in two or three instances, to portions of two volumes previously published, and to which our respondent had access. For the benefit of those who may possess these volumes, we have given references, or condensed the thought and put it into another form.

These letters, with some additional matter and a few notes, are now submitted to the public. They are respectfully commended to the consideration of those who desire to act sincerely and intelligently in relation to the matters in question. "Prove all things: hold fast that which is good," is a Scripture precept.

The matter of some of the letters has been prepared in haste. The discussion covers the living issues of our times between the friends and opponents of evangelical Christianity. The style is as popular as the character of the subjects would permit. If it shall answer the ends of a hand-book on the subject of heterodoxy in religion and reform, the author's aim will be accomplished.

LETTER I.

NONSENSE OF THEODORE PARKER'S THEOLOGICAL PHILOSOPHY.

MY DEAR SIR:

I learned to respect you for your learning and talents in by-gone years. When I first knew you I doubted concerning the divine legation of Moses and the manifestation of God in Christ. Since then you have departed in some measure from the faith which you then commended to me.

It has been matter of sincere regret to myself and others that a friend, who we believe possesses one of the best minds in the land, should no longer act with us in advancing the plan of Christ in the world. But whatever may be your convictions in relation to the divine nature of Jesus, it surprises me most of all to be informed that you listen with apparent complacency to the teachings of Theodore Parker on the subject of THEISM. Whatever regard you may have for Mr. Parker as a man and a reformer—a regard which I likewise cherish—

still I am sure you can see little but a verbiage, something like Carlyleism diluted, in the style and matter of Mr. Parker's teaching. I confess that I can not see how any one who prizes the logical faculty so highly as you do, should have any respect for such a book as the "Discourses of Religion," which has scarcely a reliable logical process from its beginning to its close.

I think you injure the character of your countrymen in the estimation of thinking men, both at home and abroad, by the sanction which a discriminating American scholar may seem to give to the vagaries of such a writer as Mr. Parker.

The course pursued by other gentlemen in relation to Mr. Parker as a public teacher, differs, in my opinion, morally, from the same course when pursued by yourself. Men who have little or no knowledge of the Scriptures, and who affiliate mostly with those who reject the authority of God in Christ, if they have sagacity to see the defection from Christian principle which exists about them, may be expected to swell the pæan which hails the anti-scriptural reformer.

But should any apparent defections in some portions of the Christian church lead such men as you to reject Christian principle?

You answer by saying that, "When Parker has the courage to denounce statesmen who prostitute their great talents, and become recreant to the principles of freedom and humanity; and when Greeley has the courage to sustain the denouncement, although it is against his own party—or rather against a self-degraded man who was the Magnus Apollo of his own party—the man," you say, "whose *better nature* does not sympathize with such devotion to principle, while it reluctates against those venal ministers and presses that are silent, or become the apologists for theological or political sinners, has no *better nature*."

I have, you know, no desire to abate any thing from the homage which you pay to the moral courage of reformers. I only regret that the class of men to whom you refer should reject the faith which alone can give a right spirit and final success to their efforts. So long as they reject Christ as the model and motive, they will themselves grow more selfish, and their constant failures will make them misanthropes in the end.

So far, then, as Mr. Parker and other teachers and lecturers of his class get indorsement from *you*, there is ground for that blame which always attaches to those *who know* when they sanction the transfer of a valueless or injurious article to those *who do not know.*

There are many men—young men especially—who have paid little or no attention to the grave matters which Mr. Parker "talks about," and who no doubt suppose that his scholastic words and phrases upon theological subjects have profound truth and significance in them. You know better, and should not therefore give, even by silent acquiescence, countenance to teachings which must be an offense to your intelligence if not to your conscience.

Allow me here to note for you some passages in Mr. Parker's "Discourses of Religion." They will sufficiently indicate the character of his theologizing, and warrant any language which may seem to you or others to be severe in the foregoing paragraphs:

1. THE "SENTIMENT" OF GOD.

Mr. Parker says (p. 18), "The *religious sentiment* does not disclose the character, and much less the nature and object, on which it depends."

Again (p. 27), "The *sentiment of God*, though vague and mysterious, is always the same in itself."

2. THE "IDEA" OF GOD.

On page 24 we are told that "the *idea* of God comes of the joint and spontaneous action of reason and the religious sentiment."

Again (p. 27), "The *idea* of God as a *fact* given in man's nature, and affording a consistent representation of its object, is permanent and alike in all."

But (p. 24) we are told that "The idea of God is perfect only when the conditions are complied with"—but, in a majority of cases, "the conditions are not complied with."

3. THE "CONCEPTION" OF GOD.

Page 24. "The CONCEPTION of God, as man expresses it, is always imperfect."

Page 27. "The conception of God is of the most VARIOUS and EVANESCENT character, and is not the same in any two ages or men."

Page 95. "The conception which man forms of God depends on his character."

In the above passages the italics are our own, introduced to note the points which we shall notice. The sense is fairly and fully quoted. They are "UTTERED" mostly in the same chapter, and near the beginning of the book. Taken together, their absurdity is equaled only by other "INTUITIONS" of like character which follow them in the same volume.

First, we are told that the mind of man has three different apprehensions of God, which are spoken of: SENTIMENT, IDEA, and CONCEPTION. Now, if we suppose all these to exist at the same time, as Mr. Parker evidently does, the notion is a positive absurdity. They might exist consecutively, combined with a doubt which were right; but that they should exist simultaneously as SEPARATE apprehensions, is contrary to the laws of mind.

If they could exist simultaneously, the one apprehension would nullify the other. One would be various and false, the other permanent and true; while a third would be mysterious and always the same.

But if these succeed each other—which is first, and which is most influential? Mr. Parker tells us that the conception of God is different in all men, and always imperfect. Does this "conception" obliterate the idea which is given as a FACT in man's nature? Of what benefit is a true idea if it be obliterated in all men (EXCEPT a few such men as Mr. Parker) by a conception which is utterly false? Beside, how can a sentiment—the same in all—and an idea which is a fact given in man's nature, ever be varied or perverted by a conception which is different in all men?

This SENTIMENT, IDEA, and CONCEPTION is a sort of trinity never before thought of—not a trinity in unity, but a trinity in antagonism existing in the same mind.

If man is conscious of these three different apprehensions of God, either in connection or in succession, why does he not choose one of them? But if the idea is a fact given in his nature, then he can not obliterate from his mind a true knowledge of God. And again, would not the "vagueness" of the sentiment be dissipated by the definiteness of the idea, or the force of the conception?

We are told, on page 24, that the idea of God comes of the joint and spontaneous action of *reason* and the religious sentiment (*action* of a sentiment?), but we are informed, on page 125, that this vague and indefinite sentiment, combined with ignorance and fear, *leads to superstition*. And then, on page 188, *et seq.*, man can by reason get but an imperfect knowledge from nature: yet from a vague and mysterious sentiment and imperfect data, a Being of wisdom, power, and love, is derived by the reason.

But strange enough, in immediate connection with this, the idea of God is said to be "a FACT *given in man's nature, which affords a consistent representation of its object*, PERMANENT AND ALIKE IN ALL." Thus it is at the same time an intuition, given as a fact in man's nature, permanent and alike in all, while yet it is the result of a rational process, predicated upon a vague sentiment and imperfect data.

But strange again, we are told in the same chapter that this idea, which is permanent and alike in all, "depends upon conditions which, in a majority of cases, are not complied with."

How can a fact which is the same in all, depend upon conditions? Or, if the fact be unknown until the conditions are complied with, how can any man rationally comply with the conditions of the unknown? Mr. Parker must solve such difficulties for his friends by *intuition*. They are without the limits of reason.

But the *conception* of God, as we have been informed, is very different from either the sentiment or the idea. "It is (p. 27) of the *most various and evanescent character, and is not the same in any two ages or men.*" This conception of God, we are told, "depends on a man's character;" that it is bad or good as a man is bad or good; and that it is "*always imperfect.*" But subsequently we hear something very different of this conception. On pp. 156–7, Mr. Parker analyzes it, and finds in the evanescent and imperfect conception, which is never the same in any two men, what he denominates the perfect character of God. He says: "At the end of the analysis what is left?—BEING—CAUSE—KNOWLEDGE—LOVE—each with no conceivable limitations. To express it in a word, a Being of infinite power, wisdom, and goodness. Thus, by an analysis of the *conception* of God, we find in fact, or by implication, just what was given synthetically by the intuition of the reason."

Now, as we were taught that the character of the conception depends on the character of the man, and that *it is never the same in any age or in any two men*, whose conception has Mr. Parker analyzed? And if he finds this result in one case, according to his own authority, he will certainly find a different one in every other case. And as conceptions have an objective origin, how can an analysis of a conception give an intuition as its result?

But this is not all that Mr. Parker has to teach

his hearers on the subject of the divine nature and the divine character. Such vagaries as the following occur further on in the same volume:

Page 151. "God can not be personal and conscious as Joseph and Peter, and yet impersonal and unconscious as moss," etc.

Page 159. "God is the substantiality of matter!"

Page 170. "God is the *materiality* of matter."

Page 156. "God is universal being."

This is pantheism run mad. If God is substantial, and material, and universal being, he must be developed into all specialities, such as doves and snakes, eagles and alligators, porcupines and pumpkins.

Again, page 149. "God is infinite motherliness," and "is immanent in all things."

Page 163. "The things of nature reflect his image, and make real the *conception*." Yet the conception, we are told, is of the most various and evanescent character.

On page 377, we are told that "we can only know God through self;" but, strange to say, the contrary of this is likewise true, for on page 392 we are informed that "there is nothing but self between us and God."

Even these are not the worst passages as specimens of Parkerism. There are others in which transcendental verbiage becomes worse than ridiculous. As that on page 140, where it is written, "Nature, which is the *outness* of God, favors religion, which is the *inness* of man; and so God works with us. Heathens knew it many centuries ago."

Now, we affirm that this is not true, and we postulate its antagonism thus: "Theodore Parker, who is the *upness* of materialism, favors diluted moonshine, which is the *inness* of transcendentalism; thus mental charlatanism works with us, and men of discernment knew it years ago."

In all the attributes of nonsense, the first paragraph is more than a match for the second one. I am almost ashamed to put such rhodomontade upon paper, but I am more ashamed of my countrymen, who hear and laud it.

There are, likewise, in this book evidences of malignity toward the sacred writers and the orthodox faith, which I am sorry to see, and which give a darker hue to its spirit than that given by conceited or erratic intellect. On page 275 Mr. Parker speaks of the Evangelists as "*dull evangelists*," who may have thrust their own *fancies* into the mouth of Jesus; and on page 277 he says Christ did not call Peter "a false liar, *as he was*."

Now that a man can write in this way concerning those whom Jesus called as his friends and disciples, and commissioned to be the founders of the Christian Church, and concerning one who willingly atoned for an error by penitence and martyrdom, is an indication of malignity so distinct that it is painful. It may not seem so to Mr. Parker, but it will seem so to every one who is in sympathy with the spirit and principles of Christ and his apostles. It may be said that Christ spoke of Peter as a tempter, and admonished him of his errors. But the language of admonition and rebuke serves a purpose. The language of malignity, when no good end can be subserved by it, is a different thing.

I have written these paragraphs to establish a principle. I have used Mr. Parker's name and his book, rather as the representatives of a class. If Mr. Parker would accept revelation as a guide to his reason, and the example and spirit of Christ as model and impulse in the achievement of all real good for humanity, he would be a wiser and a better man. The man who rejects these, and yet professes to teach of God and duty, is necessarily a BLIND LEADER of the BLIND.

LETTER II.

VARIATIONS AND INCONGRUITIES.

My Dear Sir :—

How is it that such men as you tolerate dogmatic assertion and crude philosophisms in such writers as Carlyle, Emerson, and Parker, while on the same subject you require in others mature and accurate thought? It is possible that in relation to some things the teachings of Christ may not be fully nor clearly apprehended, even by those who receive and obey his instruction; thoughtfully to examine those teachings is therefore lawful and proper. If there be objections to the views of Christians, let them be distinctly and fairly stated, and upright minds will hear and weigh the reasons alleged by objectors. If men have a better system to propound, let them show it, and old errors will vanish in the light of a newly-developed truth. Let those who do not discriminate between good sense and pompous pretense stand agape in the presence of theological bravado and assertion; but will you, and the intelligent class of men to which you belong, accept crude *dicta* from any man, on a subject of serious moment, and accept it, as I am sorry to believe, with little or no examination.

We do not design, in thus writing, to disparage the conceded ability of the authors to whom we have alluded. In some respects they are learned and able men; and Mr. Parker, especially, seems to me to be sincerely engaged in some of the reform efforts of our time. But any mind—even that of Laplace or Bishop Butler—were it afloat on the sea of skeptical conjecture, without the pole-star by which reason might direct her course, would become perplexed, and would perplex others, by its erratic wanderings on a starless sea.

Notice, with me, whether there be any evidence of crude and contradictory thought in the teachings of the popular skeptic already named:—

Mr. Parker affirms that "Christianity is the absolute religion," and that Jesus taught absolute religion to men. Now, this is obviously true, and when rightly considered, it is *absolute evidence*, not only of the divine origin, but of the divine nature of Christianity. Christianity teaches absolute obedience to God. It reveals infinite love in Christ. Love can reach an expression no higher than is given in the crucifixion. It is in Christ stronger than death—hence it is absolute. The Fatherhood of God—the brotherhood of men are taught in ultimate and absolute terms. Filial obedience becomes absolute when we love God with all our heart; and righteousness is absolute when we love our neighbor as ourself. There can be nothing different—nothing better—nothing further in morals and piety than the example and teachings of Christ: hence Christianity, as expressed by the life and teachings of Jesus, is absolute and ultimate religion.

We may affirm that Christianity is absolute in another sense. It is perfectly and alone adapted to promote the highest good of men. If received and obeyed in the spirit of its Author, it combines as much of happiness and active usefulness in the life of its recipient as his constitution will permit.

Let it be allowed, then, in the accepted sense, that Jesus taught the absolute religion. In this the true Christian rejoices. This Mr. Parker affirms; but yet, as we shall see, he makes his own statement both nugatory and ridiculous.

Mr. Parker says, in the beginning of his book, p. 18, that "*the religious sentiment does not itself disclose the character*, and still less the nature and essence, of the object on which it depends."

Again, p. 27—"The sentiment of God, though vague and mysterious, is always the same in itself."

Further, on p. 226, we are told that "Christianity can be no greater than the religious sentiment, though it may be less."

The absolute religion of Mr. Parker, then, is no greater than a *vague* sentiment, that does not itself disclose the character of God—"and it may be less." Verily, Mr. P.'s disciples are in the way of getting a queer idea of "the absolute religion" taught by Jesus.

But furthermore, there is not only one, but there are several judges to aid in deciding that "Christianity is the absolute religion." On p. 22, we are informed that "Christianity is to be judged of by the religious sentiment—by other forms of religion, and by reason." Strange enough, this—a religion to be judged by a vague sentiment that does not give the character of God! Christianity does give the character of God. How shall it be judged by a sentiment that does not? How shall facts be judged by a sentiment! But Mr. P.'s absolute religion is not only to be judged by reason, which is well enough (if he means enlightened reason), but it is to be judged by other religions. We supposed the absolute was the judge of all else; but Mr. P. makes all else judge the absolute.

We are told, on p. 269, of a peculiarity of the absolute religion which Mr. P. teaches, and tells his readers Jesus of Nazareth taught. He says:

"It is not a system of theological or moral doctrines, but a method of religion and life. *It lays down no positive creed to be believed in—commands no positive action to be done.* It would make man perfectly obedient to God, leaving his thoughts and actions for reason and conscience to govern."

We have, then, an absolute Christianity which is a method without theological or moral doctrines. What does Mr. P. intend to do with his theological doctrine of the religious sentiment? He tells us, too, at the close of his book, that he wants "real Christianity—the absolute religion—preached with faith, and applied to life." Faith in what? A doctrine is a rule of faith and practice; but if "Christianity has neither theological or moral doctrine" in it, and requires neither faith nor practice, how can it be preached with faith?—how applied to life? Does not Mr. P. mean a *transcendental* rather than an *absolute* religion. We think this must be so, as the same author teaches in another volume (Ten

Sermons, p. 12), that a man may be religious and not know it.

Mr. P. tells us that his absolute religion is a "method of life according to conscience and reason." But a man's conscience is as his faith; and we are told that the absolute religion of Mr. Parker prescribes no creed to be believed. The method, then, must be very various; and it can not be a method of any particular value, for our philosopher tells us, in another place (p. 104), that "many a savage—his hands smeared all over with human sacrifices—shall come from the east and the west, and sit down in the kingdom of God, with Moses and Zoroaster, with Socrates and Jesus." The worst method in the world, then, will answer the same end as Mr. Parker's Christian method. And then Mr. Parker tells us, that method is all there is of Christianity! O transcendentalism!

Mr. Parker's "absolute Christianity," then, is a religion no greater, but which may be less, than a vague religious sentiment. It offers nothing to be believed. It commands nothing to be done. It is a method of life; but any other method—even a human sacrifice—will answer the same end!

There are other definitions of "absolute Christianity," some of which are better than the foregoing.

It would be wrong to pass them without notice. In one place we are told, religion is "perfect obedience to the law of God, revealed in *instinct, reason, conscience*, and the *religious sentiment*." The Mormons have this phase of the absolute, putting *instinct* first, as Mr. Parker does.

There is another definition on page 226, which approaches the circle of sense, and if the author would admit that "faith which works by love," his definition on this page might be accepted. He says, "Absolute religion is perfect obedience to the law of God"—"perfect love toward God and man exhibited in a life allowing and *demanding* a harmonious action of all man's faculties so far as they act at all."

This, although a little blind as to its import, is a very different thing from the absolute religion on another page, which proposes nothing to be believed, and requires nothing to be done.

Then, on page 271, we have something just the opposite of what is said before. We are told that "Christianity differs from other religions in its eminently *practical character*." Agreed, Mr. Parker! Eminently practical, certainly, if we take the life and teachings of the Christ as its exponent. Let us forget the falsehood and folly of "nothing to be believed and nothing commanded," and listen to the voice of the Master calling us to faith and duty—"Go ye, therefore, teach all nations, baptizing them in the name of the FATHER, and of the SON, and of the HOLY GHOST—teaching them to *observe all things whatsoever I have* COMMANDED *you*, and lo! I am with you always, even to the end of the world. Amen."

There, my dear sir! How different the intent, the thought, and the spirit of this commission from the theological vagaries over which we have passed! The doctrine of the Trinity—*one* name, yet three persons; men to be baptized into that three persons in one name; taught to "observe all things that Christ had commanded," with the blessed promise annexed of the spiritual presence of Jesus: "Lo! I am with you always unto the end of the world."

What is this? Christ a man like his disciples, and yet to be with them, everywhere and always, unto the end of the world!

Pausing and thoughtful—your friend as ever.

LETTER III.

MISSTATEMENTS.

MY DEAR SIR:—

Men who are sincere and interested inquirers in relation to religious truth, will not commit themselves to a guide who, by any subterfuge, exhibits part of the truth as the whole—certainly not to one who makes exaggerated and erroneous statements in relation to the facts in the case. Honest men sometimes misrepresent the opinions of others because they are not fully informed upon the subject of discussion; but erroneous statements are inexcusable when they are made by those who seek to gain an end by perverting, or keeping out of sight, a correct view of the subject which they are opposing. This bad men, who are political or religious partisans, will do; but this a man who honestly seeks to discover and establish truth will not do.

In the volume before us there is evidence of

subterfuge and erroneous affirmation. Let us put the best construction upon the motive, while we notice some palpable instances.

In speaking of inspiration in the general sense—or of "the influence of God in nature," to use the language of the author (p. 212)—the lovely, the interesting—whatever leaves upon the sense a pleasant impression, or stirs the mind with elevating thought, is grouped into a picture to convey an idea of God, as he exhibits himself to the senses; and then we are told, "Nature is religion." But the "night side of nature" is omitted. It is indeed pleasant to ignore foul odors, poison, torture, malignant passion, and the horrid and the driveling in natural objects; but for one possessing Mr. Parker's opinions—one who involves the divine in the material—for such an one to speak of God in natural good, while he omits to notice in the same connection natural evil, is simply to beguile such of his hearers as choose to be thus beguiled; and such likewise as are unable to discriminate between rhetoric and reason.

In "Discourses of Religion," p. 239, Mr. Parker states that Jesus considered himself as sent of God, but he adds, "Yet he never speaks of his connection with God as peculiar; never calls himself the Son of God in any sense wherein all good men are not also sons of God."

Now, this statement is an absolute misrepresentation of the teaching of Christ. Can it be that Mr. Parker would take advantage of the ignorance of many of his readers in relation to the claims of the Redeemer? Shall we not rather suppose that the writer's zeal to gain a point had excluded, for the time being, from his mind all counter statements?

Jesus says, Matt. xi. 27, and also in Luke, "*All things are delivered to me of my Father; and no man knoweth who the Son is, but the Father, and who the Father is, but the Son, and he to whom the Son will reveal him.*"

Here the Christ not only speaks of himself as sovereign of *all things,* but he affirms that no one knows who or what he is, but the Father; and further, that no man knows the Father but the Son, *and he to whomsoever the Son will reveal him.*

Notice, Christ, as the Son, is the revealer of the Father. And without the revelation which Christ makes, no man knows who God the Father is. And notice, especially, that *he declares his own nature to be still more unknown to men* than that of the Father. The Father only knows the Son, but it is *not said* the Father reveals the Son. The Son only knows the Father, but *it is said* the Son reveals the Father. The union of God with humanity in Christ is a mystery, as it respects the nature of that union.

Instead, therefore, of its being true that Christ never speaks of himself as holding a peculiar connection with the Father, differing from that of other good men, he affirms the awakening truths that the Father alone knows the Son, and that the Son alone knows the Father; and that he is the only revealer of the Father to men.

Now, my dear sir, what shall we think of our countrymen who assail the divine in Christianity under the guidance of a champion who makes such palpable misstatements in regard to one of the most vital points involved in the subject of inquiry?

To the foregoing might be added many passages from the book of John, which I am just informed this author has recently concluded does not belong to the Apostolic age. Matthew and Luke, however, are yet, I presume, considered evangelists, although Mr. Parker speaks of them as being "dull," and often mistaken.

There are flippant and false charges against the orthodox religion in this volume. In the Introduction it is written, "The popular religion is hostile to man; tells us he is an outcast; not a child of God; but a spurious issue of the devil." Now it was Jesus who said, "Ye are of your father the devil, and the lusts of your father ye will do" (John, viii. 44). In the sense in which Jesus uttered these words the statement is true, and the popular religion never makes the statement in any other sense.

The tonor of the gospel, as taught by all evangelical preachers, is just the opposite of what Mr. Parker would convey by these words. While it teaches that all men are the servants of sin, and not characteristically children of God, yet this is made the very basis of mercy. God, in the person of his Son, speaks to the offenders—offers pardon—enlightens the mind by truth—does not impute sin where there is no light—and with the light there is revealed a love that is stronger than death, in order to subdue the heart to the rule of duty. And then eternal life is promised to all who, being enlightened, will repent from sin, and love God in Christ, and thus be induced to labor for the good of men." (See "God Revealed in Creation and in Christ," p. 299, etc.) This is the teaching of the gospel, according to the popular religion, and yet our author tells his readers that this religion is hostile to man! They manifest hostility to man who labor to turn away his mind from this religion. We hope such may be forgiven. "They know not what they do."

It would be utterly impracticable to go through the book and mark all the passages which offend against truth and fairness, in a manner similar to those noted above. Mr. Parker is adroit in weaving into the same passage—often into the same paragraph—a mixture of truth and error. Sometimes one predominates, and sometimes the other. In relation to the life and death of Christ, he writes plainly. After affirming that the party he represents "calls God Father, not King," and "Religion nature," with various other expressions equally right and wrong, hes ays—"*Jesus lived for himself, died for himself, worked out his own salvation*, and we must do the same, for one man can not live for another any more than he can eat or sleep for him."

This sort of guileful sophistry, to give it no worse name, is prevalent throughout the book. "One man can not live for another any more than he can eat or sleep for him!" Suppose I should say, one man can not succor or instruct another any more than he can breathe for him! Can not men of sense see the fallacy of such statements? To eat and sleep are the habitudes of the animal nature, necessary to the existence of animal life. But do not parents, in a moral sense, often live for their children?—work for them—suffer for them—nay, even die for them? One man can not eat for another, but one man can procure food to sustain life in others who have no means of procuring it for themselves. This Mr. Parker *knows* is the sense of the New Testament. And shall one earthly friend suffer and even die for another, while our Divine Friend and Father will not manifest so much love for his earthly children?

It is said that a Scotchman, whose wife, for some offense against the laws, was sentenced to undergo certain penal labors—labors more than he supposed her little strength could endure—obtained the release of his wife by discharging the penalty which was to be inflicted on her. Did he not live for her—bear her burden? And would not his wife abhor the offense ever afterward which brought the evil on her husband?—a husband now rendered surpassingly dear to her by the manifestation of his love; and would she not avoid a repetition of the offense, and love him with the love of devotion and gratitude to the end of her days?

As human nature is constitued by its Maker, this would be the effect upon the human heart of such acts of self-denial for the benefit of the guilty. And the very nature of love, of goodness, of mercy, is to impart of our means, our efforts, and even of our blood, if need be, for the good of our fellow-men. Love is absolute. It is one. It must be the same in kind in God as in man. It is one in all moral beings. Holy minds find their life and happiness in the labor and self-denial which love prompts for the good of others. Is not God benevolent? If he is, then love begets love; and hence an exhibition of self-denying love for men would aid and bless all who would believe. Manifested love reconciles enemies. Would not God manifest his love to the disobedient? Would he himself act according to laws which himself has constituted? If Christ's sacrifice was not an exhibition of divine love, then God is not so benevolent as he requires man to be. Has heaven manifested no benevolence to earth? Not if Mr. Parker's statement be true. If "*Christ lived for himself and died for himself*," there is benevolence on earth, but not in heaven.

"Christ died for Himself," says Mr. Parker. Did he? Then he did what he did not intend to do. He says, in Matthew, xx. 28, "The son of man came not to be ministered unto, but to minister; *and to give his life a ransom for many.*" So believers and confessors have ever *understood* and *felt* in relation to Christ's death. "He gave himself a ransom for all to be testified [made known to all] in due time." "He worked out his own salvation," says Mr. Parker. Did he? Then he did what he did not mean to do. He affirms that "for your sakes I sanctify myself, that you may be sanctified through me." He said he should "be lifted up, that whosoever believeth on him might not perish, but have everlasting life." "*The good shepherd giveth his life for the sheep.*"

Here, my dear sir, I leave this portion of the book which you commended to my notice. Its teachings I pronounce to be untrue to Scripture, and often false to reason. Its style is sinister and pretentious. Its teachings are as unlike the Christianity of the New Testament as your beautiful garden is unlike the tangled morass where grow some wild-flowers, but flowers enveloped in impure vapor. The flowers are those aspects of reform and humanity for which we respect the author—the vapors are the prevalence of wrong and hurtful thought, which we deplore.

At some time not far in the future I shall notice some other things in this work, and endeavor to give you my views of the reasonableness of some of the fundamental doctrines of Christianity—especially of those doctrines which are rejected by the prevailing skepticism of our times.

Yours truly.

LETTER IV.

DIVINE PERSONALITY.

My Dear Sir:—

The skepticism of our times, like its talented preachers, is popular in many circles of well-informed people. I call it *skepticism,* because, while it assails the generally-received faith of evangelical Christians, it offers no comprehensible system instead of the faith it labors to destroy. It begets doubt, but it produces no conviction that is influential upon the heart and will of men. It is, therefore, *skepticism;* and if the Christian religion, in its evangelical interpretation, be of any value, it is hurtful skepticism.

It is popular in some instances, because it assumes the attitude of reform, and therefore commends itself to minds of humane and progressive tendencies. It is popular in a wider sense with many who desire to retain the name of Christian while they refuse obedience to Christ. In the name of Jesus it denies the divine authority of Christianity; whether a man receive or reject the gospel, he is a Christian: he that believeth shall be saved, and he that believeth not shall be saved. Such a system has the elements of popularity with all sorts of men, except those who maintain the Scripture doctrine, that repentance and faith in the Lord Jesus Christ are conditions of holiness and eternal life.

But does this modern phase of skepticism commend itself to the reason of fair-minded men? Should the doubts which it encourages concerning the foundational truths of revealed religion be entertained? Let us put into the balance of reason some of its utterances, and weigh them against the doctrines of the Christian faith.

You will, doubtless, have noticed, that while the writers of the Carlyle school, such as Emerson and Parker, adopt language which speaks of God as a personal being, they likewise write many passages which make the impression that there is no personal God; or none that can be called personal in any comprehensible sense. On this, as on other subjects of the most grave interest, one may find on one page of Mr. Parker's book a distinct recognition of truth, while in another place the same truth is perplexed by doubt, nullified by contradictory expressions, or rendered incomprehensible by words as innocent of any particular import as moonshine is of caloric.

We have noticed, in a preceding letter, the peculiar philosophy in relation to the "idea," "sentiment," and "conception" of God. Now, if any of Mr. P.'s disciples suppose that by this teaching they know any thing about God as a personal being, there are several passages that will correct that mistake at once. It had been said that all men have an idea of God; but, according to other passages, if any one believes that he knows any thing about God, either as a *personal* or a *conscious* divine being —or that he has any comprehensible "idea" whatever on this subject, it is all a mistake. Notice this in the following passage:

"We *talk* of a personal God. If thereby we only deny that he has the limitations of unconscious matter, no harm is done. But our conception of personality is that of finite personality, limited by human imperfections—hemmed in by time and space—restricted by partial emotions—displeasure —wrath—ignorance—caprice. Can this be said of God? If matter were conscious, as Locke thinks (?) it possible, it must predicate materiality of God, as persons predicate personality. If it mean God has not the limitations of our personality, it is well. But if it mean that he has those of unconscious matter, it is worse than the other term. *Can God be personal and conscious as Joseph and Peter—unconscious and impersonal as a moss or the celestial ether?* No man will say it. Where, then, is the philosophic value of such terms?"—p. 151.

Now, we affirm that this is not only directly contradictory to what was said before, but that there is neither philosophy nor sense in it.

Mr. Parker, as we have seen, analyzes the conception which he says men form of God, and finds in it "power, wisdom, and love," *without limitation.* Now, if the idea of personality in God must be limited by human imperfection, why not wisdom and love thus limited? There is contradiction in affirming the one and denying the other. So that, if Mr. P. affirms that God is not personal in any comprehensible sense, then he must affirm, according to his own showing, that God is neither wise nor unwise, good nor evil, in any comprehensible sense. To affirm personality of God as an infinite being is, as we shall see, more rational than to affirm wisdom or love of him, because the human idea of *moral character*, without revelation, is imperfect; but the idea of personal identity is absolute, and always the same in all beings.

There are some things which are the same in themselves, and the same forever. Truth must be the same to all intelligent beings, so far as known to them. Two and three are five with God as they are with Joseph and Peter. Self-consciousness can not be one thing in God and another thing in man. The absolute truths of the universe, when known, must be the same to all beings that have a moral nature, or else the moral universe is founded on the principle of discord. Personality is an absolute truth—it is an intuition. We conceive of it in God as distinctly as we perceive it in ourselves.

Mr. Parker's reasons, annexed to the above paragraph, are about equal to the reasons annexed to his statements on some other subjects. So far as there is any reason in the matter, the author's idea is, that because God can not be affirmed to be impersonal and unconscious as the moss and the celestial ether, therefore he is not personal nor conscious. If the argument were good for any thing—judging of the cause from the effect—then, as two opposite characteristics are instanced in the objects named, instead of proving that God is neither conscious nor unconscious, personal nor impersonal, it would prove that he is both the one and the other. The foregoing passage is written in the phrase of blank pantheism; and yet Mr. Parker, in other places, denies the doctrine.

Furthermore, it is admitted by the writer that man is a personal and conscious being, and that matter is not personal or conscious. It is conceded that personal agents and impersonal objects do exist. To deny this would be to deny the validity of both sense and reason. Now, if it be a fact that personal and conscious agents do exist, *separate* from impersonal and unconscious objects, why may not God exist as a proper personal and conscious being, separate from and ruling over the kingdoms of nature? Is man a personal and conscious being, while God has a mixed identity—conscious and unconscious at the same time! To argue that because one man is white and another is black, therefore George Washington could be neither a white man nor a black man, would be a conclusion as rational as that of Mr. P. when he utters the nonsense, that because personal agents and impersonal objects both exist, therefore God is neither, or that he is both.

To doubt of the personality of God and his conscious separateness from matter, is to plunge the human reason back into the blindness of an atheistic philosophy. The wisdom of the ancients, of which Plato is the highest exponent, after ages of discussion, reached the conclusion that plan was before organization—a designer before a construction. And if there be such a thing as an intuition (which we ought to admit, notwithstanding the word is sadly abused by the transcendentalists when they utter their opinions in its name), this is one—the designer is before and apart from the design. Man is conscious of designing and then of moulding the unconscious matter into the forms of the mental archetype. We are so made, that it is not possible for any one to perceive clearly the marks of design in any object without the accompanying conviction that plan was before the construction. Whether we call this conviction, intuition, experience, or a logical deduction, the result is still the same: common reason teaches every man, what philosophy sanctions as the result of her most profound inquiries, that a designing cause is before and apart from a designed effect. Reason affirms design in nature. To write skeptically, therefore, concerning the conscious personality of God, as Mr. Parker has done, is a sin against reason and philosophy, as well as against common sense and religion.

But there are scientific facts, ascertained beyond question, which should dispel the vague notions of those who speak of God as the "materiality of matter," and as being "inseparable from nature." An extract from "God Revealed in the Process of Creation, and by the Manifestation of Christ," will, I think, show that the idea of a God who is neither conscious nor unconscious, in the common acceptation of language, is no more in consonance with the facts of science than it is with the deductions of right reason.

The "Natural Development" theory—which argues that nature has been advanced from lower to higher species, by some law or power which is inseparable from the material universe, and which has developed itself from inanimate matter up through an ascending series from the lowest to the highest genera of things—issues itself in an utter absurdity. "God is inseparable from nature," says the author of the "Vestiges." To this agree Compté and probably such philosophers as Nott, Gliddon, and multitudes of others, like Mr. Parker, who know little or nothing of the scientific basis of the argument.

Let us notice some legitimate results of this theory. The whole subject is discussed at length in the volume referred to. The following is a passage from chapter viii.:

"When it is said, 'God can not be separated from nature,' while at the same time he is affirmed to be the 'author and sustainer of nature,' the import can not be, according to this theory, that God has exercised any personal act of creation or control, since gravitation first affected the material which formed our system; or, if the theory be confined to the earth, then no creative act has been put forth by the Maker since the first organic cell was formed, and that was not formed by a divine author, but by law. God is declared to be 'nature.' It is said he is inseparable from nature, and that nature is the manifestation of God. Hence, as a logical necessity, natural phenomena, organic and inorganic, manifest all the God that belongs to this theory.

"If, then, God be inseparable from material nature now, he has been inseparable from nature in all periods of past progress. Then what follows? Why this: Reason is a product of material development; hence, before the existence of organic forms, there was no reason in existence, none, at least, in any wise connected with our planet. Intelligence was developed from lower susceptibilities up to higher instincts, and thence still up to the human mind. Then, as a sequent of this doctrine, at early periods of creative progress by law, intelligence did not exist; and if God can not be separated from nature, then before nature produced intelligence, there was no intelligent God. During the Saurian Age, the lizard mind was the highest in existence; and if there be nothing above and separate from nature, then the fish-lizard-god was, for the time, the supreme being; or at least the supremest being that acted in connection with the earth.

"But, is it said that not only the laws and beings of our earth, but the laws and beings of our whole system, or of the universe, are included in the idea of 'progressive development,' and that, with this enlarged conception, God can not be separated from nature? Now, admitting the idea to be expanded, then, if God can not be separated from nature, *He is in different stages of development in the universe at the same time.* He is in different stages of development at the same time in our solar system; thus, in either view, the idea is an absurdity.

The legitimate ultimatum of any theory that recognizes the law of progressive development in creation as a power developing new and higher species out of lower ones; and which affirms at the same time that 'God is nature' and 'inseparable from nature'—thus placing divine interposition out of the question—the ultimatum of such a theory is, that as law has produced new species progressively from the mollusk to the man, so the future will be as the past; the latter product rising above previous ones, *until the laws of nature will create a God, instead of God creating nature.*

"What a rest to the soul is the rational, philosophical, and scriptural view, compared with such atheistic monstrosities:—matter and its properties in the beginning; force developed and laws instituted by the dispositions of matter; organic life and progress from lower to higher forms; that progress effected by the *instrumentality* of natural forces and laws; advance by the destruction of lower and the introduction of higher species;—the whole *produced, advanced,* and *controlled* in accordance with a *plan* which bears the impress of a Supreme Creator and Governor."

There are moral considerations connecting themselves with this subject which add to the difficulties of skepticism, while they accumulate proofs of the personal existence of the Divine Being.

Reason can account for things as they are, only upon one of three theories.

1. Chance, or the undetermined succession of

events, in which nothing is settled, but every thing happens fortuitously and without design.

2. An omnipotent fate or law, sometimes called necessity, or the necessity of things, which causes and determines each event to exist invariably as it does; and which must thus cause all events in matter and mind forever.

3. A supreme intelligent Creator and Lawgiver, who governs the universe by laws adapted to the nature of things.

The first of these theories needs no discussion.

The second theory has been proposed by skeptical inquirers ever since the birth of philosophy. It is still held in some form by atheists, by materialists, by those who believe in a law-soul of the world; and more recently by some who seem to believe that the machine of the universe being started, its own impulse produces all phenomena and all results which are exhibited in the worlds of matter and of mind.

Supposing this theory to be true, what do we learn concerning the moral character of God, and the condition and prospects of man?

If there be no personal God, then Theodore Parker is a personal creature without a personal creator—a child without a father, and an effect without a cause. But leaving laconics which need explanation, it will not be denied that man is a mortal and dependent being. He did not cause his own existence, and he is liable at any moment to suffer detriment in mind and body by laws or circumstances (call them what you will) over which he has no control. If there be no personal God who administers a moral government which differs from the allotments of nature, then man is plainly the victim of a power that is malignant in its nature. Call that power what you will—the "substantiality of matter," as Parker would say; or the impersonal nature of things, as Mirabaud and Compté would assert. A personal God separate from nature being ignored, then the nature of things is a power—man is subject to that power, and that power is evil *per se*, and evil in development. If this blind power be called God, it can be described by adding a single adjective to the definition of Mr. Parker—a "God—neither personal nor impersonal, conscious nor unconscious"—but *malignant.*

In order to see the ground of this affirmation, notice in connection with it the phenomena of conscience.

If all things occur by a force of nature, or by any impersonal force operating through nature, a man should suffer no more for an evil act than a good one. If a parent were to force, or even influence his child to do a certain action, and then punish him for doing it, such a father would be a monster. It has been replied to this, that a man suffers compunction of conscience because he *believes* an act to be wrong, and thus believing, it is *righteousness*, in the nature of things, which causes him to suffer for it. But evidently this reply only removes the difficulty one step further back. According to this system, a man's faith, good or bad, is produced as much by a force of nature and circumstance as his actions; hence, the compunction of conscience is still the result of a necessitated antecedent. Nature, therefore, which attaches remorse to an act which she herself produces, either immediately or by a chain of causes, is just as malignant as a parent would be if he influenced his son to do a wrong action and then punished him for doing it. If man be a voluntary moral agent, and sin a moral evil, the office of conscience in admonishing of sin and denouncing the sinner, is an evidence of the mercy and justice of God. But if man be not a personal agent—if God be not a personal sovereign—the conscience is a mystery and a malignity.

It is, moreover, a law of man's moral nature that the more he loves evil, and the more frequently he sins, the less he suffers from the inflictions of conscience. If, then, there be beyond this *law of nature* no God who is the moral governor and judge of men, then nature is evidently malignant; because many men grow more selfish and wicked till they die, and the more evil they become, the less remorse they feel for sin. Nature thus makes sin the way of life. Despots succeed in crushing out light and liberty by banishing the master-spirits of the age, and shedding rivers of human blood—as those heartless adventurers the Bonapartes (and, I had almost written, some of their biographers). And yet, thousands of widows and orphans suffer thousands of times more in consequence of their evil acts than they do themselves. Who dare say that if this be the work of nature, beyond which there is no God, that nature is not malignant? In charity we accept some of Mr. Parker's best definitions as his prevailing idea of God; but when he becomes a materialist with Mirabaud, or a pantheist or law-soulist with Chambers and Compté, then, instead of writing down his impersonal God as knowledge, love, power, he should write *power, law, malignity.*

But furthermore, and finally, and conclusively, unless the Maker has incorporated a falsehood into the human soul, man is a free, responsible agent, and God is a personal moral governor. Man is so constituted, that he can not feel guilty for wrong unless he is conscious that he was voluntary in the wrong act. If, therefore, he is not the responsible cause of his own moral action, God has placed a lying witness in his soul.

But look again at the irrefragible testimony which the human consciousness gives of the responsibility of man and the personality of God. Man is actually so constituted, as a moral being, that obedience and gratitude can be exercised *only toward a personal being*—a being who consciously and voluntarily does us good. Can man be grateful to the bread that satisfies his hunger? Can he obey, as a responsible being, *something* that is neither personal nor impersonal in any comprehensible sense? The thought is preposterous! Unless the moral nature of man be a lie, produced by malignity, there is a personal conscious God, in the proper and only import of those terms, to obey and love whom is the life and adaptation of the human soul.

Is it not ridiculous, as well as preposterous, to

think of Mr. Parker expatiating upon the nature of God with the exhortation to love and obedience which must follow. He tells his hearers—"God is the ground of nature"—"he is what is *permanent* in the *passing*—what is real in the apparent." "God is the materiality of matter," so "he is the spirituality of spirit." But "he is neither personal nor conscious, like Peter and Joseph, nor impersonal and unconscious, like the moss or the ether." "The greatest religious souls can say with an old heathen, 'Since God can not be fully declared by any one name, though compounded of never so many, therefore he is rather to be called by every name, he being both one and all things.'" Mr. Parker then adds an exhortation, thus: "As I have always told you, my friends, love and obedience to God is the duty and happiness of man. You have heard my description of 'the dear God.' I enjoin upon you to love and obey The Materiality of Matter, the All Things, the Spirituality of Spirit, the neither personal nor impersonal, conscious nor unconscious God. Yea, my hearers, I say unto you obey it! It is immanent in all things—in the blush of the rose and in the bite of the dog—in the breath of the breeze and in the howl of the maniac. Remember, too, our party 'calls religion nature' (p. 450)—believes 'the divine incarnation is in all mankind' (p. 451)—'asks no forgiveness for sin' (452)—therefore we will imitate the divine incarnation, and if we sin we will ask no forgiveness. Amen and amen."

Now, if this be preposterous, it is so because it is an application of Parkerism in the light of common sense. If any one says that passages are so clustered together as to make them seem preposterous, we deny the impeachment. Other results may be obtained by inferences from other passages, but the above is a fair and an unavoidable result from one class of passages written in this volume.

And beside, there are single passages which are as preposterous in themselves as these are put together, and not only in this volume, but they are found in nearly all of this author's writings. In one of his Ten Sermons (p. 176), for instance, he says of a fly, "Lo! here I am an individual and conscious thing, sucking the bosom of the world." This is certainly hyperbole run mad; and is just about as ridiculous as though I should say of Theodore Parker, "Lo! there he is, an individual and conscious philosophist, sucking transcendentalism from the great toe of the—man in the moon."

Such nonsense produced by a man of ability, capable of writing sensibly and consistently, is only another evidence that without faith the mind is like a ship without ballast, driven by contrary winds. Turn away, my dear sir, from such hallucinations—hallucinations that mingle the evil and the incongruous with something of good; and rejoice with me in the evidence, that above the laws of nature there presides a supreme personal God, the parent and the president of the universe.

There are other evidences beside those to which we have alluded that affirm this great truth—evidence in which all good and thoughtful men will rejoice together, although the doubts and difficulties interposed by skeptics were a thousand-fold greater than they are.

God IS just—

Because he has connected the monitions and reproofs of conscience with acts known to be wrong.

Because, if conscience be not heeded, it leaves the transgressor to grow hardened in evil; evil which in itself is incipient penalty, and which being voluntarily persisted in, becomes confirmed in the character of the transgressor.

Because motives to good, if obeyed, become more influential; if disobeyed, less so.

Because the moral constitution is so formed, that the more sinful men become, the more blind they become, both to the evil and the desert of sin.

Because evil is not only linked with sin here, but while it brings present evil, it also forms an evil character in the soul, which secures future evil.

God IS good—

Because, to include much in one thought, he has made the soul so that its best good consists in a life of love to God and to men. And as love only can beget love, God becomes *immanently personal* in Christ, in whose sacrifice he reveals his love—and thus by faith the law of love is fulfilled in all who walk not after the flesh, or natural mind, but after the Spirit.

Tell me now, my dear sir, is not such evidence, and the known practical results of the Christian faith, a satisfaction to the reason and a joy to the heart, while the brilliant vagaries of skeptical thinkers are empty and evil?

Yours, in behalf of right reason.

LETTER V.

THE TRI-UNITY OF THE DIVINE MIND.

MY DEAR SIR:—

At the close of a former letter I proposed to offer, when leisure would allow, some reasons affirmatory of the orthodox faith, with the design more especially to illustrate and defend some of the doctrines which are controverted or rejected by the skeptics of our times.

In what I shall say I do not propose to give a Scriptural exposition of these doctrines, nor to present them in the form of a dogmatic statement; nor do I propose to illustrate or confirm the symbols of any particular denomination.

Illustrations are seldom perfectly accurate; and reasons which should be limited to certain aspects of a question, may be misapplied to cover the whole subject. My design, therefore, will not be to prove the systematic form of the doctrines of which I shall speak; but to show that the evangelical interpretation of the Scriptures, as generally expressed in the formularies of the churches, has illustrative and analogical reasoning on its side. I desire to show that reason is with the evangelical system, and not against it; and that many aspects of vital Christian doctrine, as expressed in the New Testament, may be sustained by accurate deduction, and illustrated by the most profound analogies.

The subject is presented in this form, not so much for the edification of Christians, as to convince gainsayers that reason, so far as she utters her voice, is *with* us, and *against* them.

Let us look first at the doctrine of the Trinity. This doctrine is contained in the general expression that there is one God, *one name*, Jehovah, who is manifested in the Scriptures as subsisting in three divine persons, the Father, the Son, the Holy Ghost.

It is agreed that the word person is used in dogmatic theology, not because its common import conveys a perfect sense of the doctrine as revealed in the New Testament; but because it conveys a sense, *which, being defined by the phrases of the Scriptures*, gives an accurate idea. It is, moreover, the most proper, we may say *the only proper word*, because the sacred writers all use the pronouns which the laws of language require should be used in a personal sense in substitution for Father, Son, and Spirit. No other word in any language will generalize the expressions of the sacred writers. They apply the personal pronouns, as you know, to Father, Son, and Holy Spirit, while yet they give *to each* of these the attributes of the *one name*—JEHOVAH. It is easy for men to declaim against the doctrine of the Trinity, but so long as they can not deny this usage of the inspired writers, there is a Scriptural basis for the orthodox interpretation.

We affirm, then, that there is in the divine nature a basis for the tri-personal manifestation of God, and that it is only by the manifestation of God in three persons that the divine nature can be efficaciously known.*

* The Andover exposition of Schleiermacher, in the notes of Professor Stuart, affirms a basis in the divine mind for the triune manifestation of God to men; and affirms, likewise, the adaptations of this divine manifestation to the wants of humanity. "Tri-unity, according to my humble apprehension, consists in something that belongs to the Μονὰς itself, and which laid the foundations for the manifestations of *Father* and *Son* and *Spirit*."—"Who can refuse to acknowledge that either some *modification* or some *property* cf the divine nature, in *respect* to *substance* or *attribute* [general enough, certainly] led to the manifestation of the Godhead *in what we call a personal manner?*"

Dr. Bushnell, of Hartford, who gives Schleiermacherism blinded by an imperfect conception, doubts this, as he does the proper humanity of Christ. In our humble opinion, Andover is right in its

It is well known that in the age of Plato, when reason reached her culminating point among the ancients, the idea of the tri-unity of God was strikingly approximated. Now, while this fact does not prove that the depths of the divine can be fathomed by the finite human, we think it does prove that the most profound indications of the light of nature point in the direction of orthodox Christian doctrine.*

The Philonic exposition is grounded in the phra-

conception of the basis of that manifestation and of the person of the Redeemer, and Princeton is right in its announcement of the *one will* in three persons.

It has been true in times past that the fear of the power which graceless dogmatics have exercised to create odium against reason, has prevented many who love the truth from conceding the value of the elder developments of the human reason on this and kindred subjects [that of Plato and Philo, for instance]; but so long as it is true that the Alexandrine exposition of the *Logos* gives the *usus loquendi* of apostolic times—the man departs from the correct laws of interpretation who refuses to acknowledge the fact.

* The seeds of the philosophy of Philo are found in the Old Testament, while his system (if he really has one) is developed in Platonic phraseology. Philo in some passages undoubtedly attributes personality to the lógos; and it must be conceded that the Apostle John coincides in conception more nearly with Philo than he does with some symbolic expressions of later times—even of our times.

We might speak, too, of some of the most profound thinkers among the Unitarians who have intimated in impressive circumstances, and in imposing positions, a desire to be understood as approximating the Trinitarian views of the Godhead.—*See Channing and Bancroft's Addresses.*

seology of the Old Testament—the Platonic in the constitution of the human mind. Both of these bear the impress of the Maker's mind, and hence analogiés derived from these sources are founded in truth. We do not affirm that they are always rightly applied.

"The physical universe," you say, "as well as the moral, bears upon its nature the impress of the creator." Certainly it does, and those who are disposed to pantheistic notions—who tell their hearers that "nature is religion," and who find "God immanent in all things"—will, of course, favor analogies from the nature of material things to the nature of God. But when you say that "a simple monad lies at the origin of all natural phenomena," the illustration is clearly at fault. If the atomic philosophy be true, there is an infinity of atoms, and likewise a diversity in their qualities.

The elementary principles of matter may be separated the one from the other, by chemical processes, and each of these, perhaps, has a molecular constitution; but the actual economic entities of the physical world are mostly tri-unities. The elements of the phenomenal world were not created to exist in separate unities, but to combine in the forms in which matter is manifested to man. *The elementary principles prove by their affinities that they abhor absolute unity.* Some two elements, with electricity, the every-where-present spirit of matter, combine to form the character of material things, as manifested to the human sense. The earths, air, water, are trinities, or rather tri-unities. They have qualities as unities and qualities as tri-unitties. The elements of things were not designed to exist alone. They seek tri-unity in one spirit by their inherent affinities. And in tri-unity alone is nature practically adapted to humanity. Physical nature is mostly manifested by tri-unity.

The evangelical view of the Godhead does not need that we should plead this analogy in its support; but the fact that matter is manifested, in many instances, by a tri-unity, and that the nature of elementary things is such that they seek union in a trinity, and that it is only in this form that they have, for the most part, a practical value and relation to other things—this, we affirm, proves this much, viz., the analogies of the physical world are opposed to those who argue from nature, as you do, for absolute unity in the manifestation or in the nature of God. The awful solitude of one individual elementary essence is a thought against which the heart reluctates. God is a social being;

and the tri-unity of his nature alone enables us to conceive of him as such.

As you have introduced this form of illustration, suppose we look into the intellectual world, and inquire whether there are not analogies here that connect themselves with this subject?

Reason is an absolute unity. *Love* is an absolute unity. *Will* is an absolute unity. These are the same in themselves, and the same in all moral beings. They are separable from each other, and yet united in one consciousness. Human reason, love, and will, are finite, and they may be perverted in finite beings, but they are the same in their nature whether they inhere in an infinite or in a finite being.

The eldest Scripture declares that man was created in the moral image of God. To infer, therefore, the moral nature of the Maker from the moral nature of man, is not only warranted by the fact that *reason*, *will*, and *love* must be the same in kind in all beings, but it is warranted likewise by the statements of revelation. Now, while we do not find the human nature manifesting itself tri-personally, as the divine does, yet we do find humanity manifested in a tri-partite form. And thus reason has a basis in the one for accepting what is revealed concerning the other.

Man is one in nature. He is conscious of *oneness* in himself; while yet his nature is such that it can be made known or revealed to others only by a trifold manifestation. *To love* is a different thing from *to know;* and to *know* differs both from to *will* and to *love;* yet it is the one man that thinks, wills, and loves. And not only this, but while these powers of the human mind are diverse from each other, yet the whole man acts in each of them—the whole man *thinks*, *wills*, or *loves.*

We may know a man by his intellectual manifestation, while we know little or nothing of his affections and will—nothing of his moral character. This is experienced sometimes when we read an unknown author. We only know a man's nature truly when he has revealed himself to us in his threefold manifestation of intellect, sensibility, and will.

This analogy is but introductory. It does not, in my opinion, give a correct idea of the Trinity. A better analogy than this can be derived from the economy of moral natures. The logos of the mind (or the mental exercises or ideas) is not the same as the conscious I in the soul of man. Thought is born of man's conscious nature as the light is born of the sun. But in moral beings there is something that stands in the nature back of thought, and judges of its character and fitness. I see my thoughts and judge of them.* The I that sees and judges of the product of the mind is as separate from the thought, in one sense, as the subject is from the object. In their relation to each other, the one is begotten of the substance of the other; yet they are in a true sense one—one is the manifestation of the other—one is the vital *image* or *living exhibition* of the other. The unknown one in the human or in the divine nature can be made known only by this manifestation, and yet the true character of this logos, or son of the mind, is known only to the unknown one. As saith the Messiah, "No man knoweth the Son but the Father; and no man knoweth the Father but the Son, and he to whomsoever the Son will reveal him."

Again, while the logos, or conceived ideas, is neither the affections nor the will, yet will and affection are manifested through and by the intelligence. The logos is the out-birth of the moral nature, and it is through the logos that the tender-

* This thought undoubtedly possessed Richard Baxter when he advised his friends "to be none of those who shall charge with heresy all who say the three persons in the Godhead are—*God understanding himself, God understood by himself*, and God loving himself."

ness of the affection and the determination of the will are made known to others. The logos is an out-birth. Will and love are a procession of the moral nature through the logos. They are seen in the intelligence, and manifested by it.*

The Scriptural statement then may be affirmed as profoundly accordant with the analogies of nature. "In the beginning was the Word, and the Word was with God, and the Word was God."

Then there is the Word conceived, and the Word revealed or manifested.†

* We purposely, for the most part, avoid the imperfect definitions of mental philosophy, and use such words as we hope may be plain to common readers. Such as will refer each reader to his own consciousness.

† Matthew Henry, the best read in the Bible of all the commentators, has clearly conceived and distinctly stated the inspired conception in the first of John. We give the passage in full, for the benefit of any who seldom refer to this most biblical of all the commentators.

"The Chaldee paraphrase very frequently calls the Messia *the Word of Jehovah*, and speaks of many things in the Old Testament said to be done by *the Lord*, as done by the *Word* of the Lord. Even the vulgar Jews were taught that the *Word of God* was the same with God. The evangelist, in the close of his discourse (v. 18), plainly tells us why he calls Christ *the Word of God—because he is "the only-begotten Son which is in the bosom of the Father, and has declared him. Word* is two-fold; *word conceived and word uttered.*

(1.) There is the *word conceived:* that is *thought*, which is the only immediate product of the soul (all the operations of which are performed by *thought*), and it is one with the soul. Thus the second person in the Trinity is fitly called *the Word;* for he is the *first-*

Some passages from the ancients, held at the time when the primitive church was exercising the power which converted the world, will give the mode of thinking among the best men of that age.

The following beautiful passage is a true translation from the Exhortation of Clement of Alexandria to the Greeks: "The divine Logos—the Christ—was the cause of our being, and our well-being also, *for he was in God;* and now this Logos himself appears to men; the only being that ever partook of both natures, as well that of God as of man; to be the cause of all good to us. From him

begotten of the Father; that eternal wisdom which the Lord possessed, as the soul doth its thought, *in the beginning of his way*, Prov. viii. 22. There is nothing we are more sure of than *that we think*, yet nothing we are more in the dark about than *how we think;* who can declare the generation of *thought* in the soul? Surely then the generations and births of the eternal mind may well be allowed to be great mysteries of godliness, which we can not fathom, while yet we adore the depth.

(2.) There is the *word uttered*, and that is *speech.* Thus Christ is the *Word*, for by *him* God has in *these last days spoken to us* (Heb. i. 2), and has directed us to *hear him*, Matt. xvii. 5. He has made known God's mind to us, as a man's word or speech makes known his thoughts, as far as he pleases, and no farther. Christ is called that *wonderful speaker* (Dan. viii. 23), *the speaker* of things hidden and strange. He *is the Word* speaking *from* God to us, and *to God* for us. John Baptist was *the voice;* but Christ the Word; being *the Word*, he is the *Truth*, the Amen, *the faithful Witness of the mind of God.*"

we learn to live virtuously; by him we are conducted in the way of eternal life; as saith the divine apostle of the Lord, 'The love of God the Saviour was manifested to all men, instructing us in order that we having abjured all impiety and worldly desires, we might live soberly and piously in this world, expecting in blessed hope the manifestation of the glory of our great God and Saviour Jesus Christ.'"

Tertullian says: "The Greeks term that *Logos* which we translate Word, and thus our people [i. e. the Christians], for brevity sake, say, 'In the beginning the Word was with God,' though it would be more proper to say reason [or thought], since God was not speaking from the beginning, although rational. * * * Considering, therefore, and disposing by his reason, he effected his will by his Word, which thou mayest easily understand by what passes in thyself. * * * when thou conferrest silently with thine own reason."—*Tertull. adv. Praxeam*, c. v.

Says *Justin, Ap. ii.:* "It is not allowable, therefore, to think otherwise of the Spirit and the Power which is in God, than that it is the Logos, which also is the first-born of God."

"That distinction in the nature of God which

would lead to his development as Father, Son, and Holy Spirit, and which fitted him for this, existed from all eternity, and was an inseparable part of his nature; but Father, Son, and Holy Ghost, in the full sense of the economy of the gospel, *he actually was not*, until the incarnation of the Logos, and the outpouring of the Spirit had been actually completed."—*Moses Stuart.*

The origin of the conceived Word is as old as the divine mind. He was in the beginning with God—the eternally-begotten Son of the Father. But the revealed or manifested Word is no older in his relations to men than the time when the character of the mind is manifested to others by its Logos. "*No man hath seen God at any time; the only-begotten Son, which* IS *in the bosom of the Father, he hath declared him.*"

Man can embody his logos impersonally in written language, and send it thus embodied to all nations who understand the written character. Why then might not the "Word of God become flesh?" Why might not the Son of God thus become personally incarnate, so that the affections and will of the Father might be expressed in him and through him, not impersonally but personally, in life and power? The Scriptures affirm, what a true reason approves, that the Word of God did become flesh, and that Christ is the "out-shining of the Father's glory, and the express image of his person." "He that hath seen Christ hath seen the Father." The embodiment of man's logos in language is only vital with intelligence. The embodiment of the divine logos is the revealment of the "fullness of the Godhead bodily"—the logos in a nature in which can be manifested not only the intelligence but the affection and will of God.

Let us advance one step further, and look at this thought in another aspect. Jesus said to his disciples, "It is expedient for you that I go away, for if I go not away, the Holy Spirit, or Comforter, will not come unto you; but if I go away I will send him unto you; and when he is come, he will not speak of himself, but he will take of the things that belong to me, and show them unto you."

Thus the Spirit is represented not as a revealer of new truth, but as a personal procession from the Father through the Son into the hearts of believers. He takes the facts furnished by the Logos, and, by a revealment of life and love, gives efficacy (as divine power and love alone can do) to the truth as it is in Jesus. The Son is eternally-begotten of the Father—the same in nature with him, and the only revealer of the Father. The Holy Spirit comes to us in power and love, baptized in the humanities of Christ, being revealed in and through the Son. Christ furnishes the material for redemption—the facts which reveal the divine nature. The Holy Spirit applies them in the soul. Hence, Christ and the Holy Spirit dwelling in believers are interchangeable terms in the New Testament. The Father and the Son are likewise interchangeable. "I am in the Father and the Father in me." So "the grace of our Lord Jesus Christ, and the love of God the Father, and the communion of the Holy Ghost," are with those who believe. Such, undoubtedly, is the apostolic conception.

Let us look again into the human consciousness, and listen again to the voice of reason, while we consider revealed truth in another aspect.

Human nature, as constituted by its Maker, would certainly be fitted to appreciate the divine character. The moral relations between God and man, the one being a sovereign, the other a subject, require this; and the fitness of things observable throughout the creation, assure us of the fact. An argument, therefore, for the trinity may be found in its adaptations to the mental constitution and moral necessities of man. Let us inquire then for the value of the doctrine as adapted to meet the finite apprehension of men, and to aid them in approximating a knowledge of the character of God.

The mind of man has a logical conformation. It is made to ratiocinate, to develop processes of synthesis, analysis, and generalization. In studying the nature of any thing, we combine its manifestations, or phenomena, and thus gain a knowledge of its true character. This being the character of the mind, it is adapted by its constitution to attain ultimate knowledge of God through the revealed doctrine of the Trinity, in the same way by which it attains knowledge of other things, that is, *by the exercise of its rational powers*. If the knowledge of God's *character*, as well as his *being*, were by intuition, as Mr. Parker teaches, man would not know the character of God as a reasoning being, but as an unreasoning animal.

The character of God is adapted to *regenerate* nature, and adapted to *regenerated* nature; hence man's rational nature is profoundly adapted to the doctrine of the Trinity. The mind of man can not apprehend the divine character, nor the relations of God to his creatures, by a single conception. Even the character and relations of an earthly ruler can not be compassed by one view of the mind. Victoria is not only *Regina*, but she is Defender of the Faith and patroness of the great charities of her queendom. (We speak of Victoria because she is a rare instance of a virtuous sovereign, while she combines in her person regal, spiritual, and benevolent prerogative.) In order to form a true idea of the character of this sovereign, and of her relations to her realm, we must form the distinct conception of three regal offices, and of the queen acting *personally* in each of these, and then combine these several conceptions in one character.* By this illustration we do not, of course, mean to be understood that the Christ-hood is only God acting officially: while this is true, yet it is, as we have shown, also true that Christ is Logos—the revealer of the Godhead bodily and personally. The statement is presented to prove a fact which is verified in the experience of every man—(a fact, the consideration of which ought to influence the mind of skeptics to a right conclusion)—that the mind of man is so constituted, that the triune

* It would, perhaps, be more proper to say that person is an intuition or coetaneous conception always present in the mind when we conceive of a moral being; and the three offices attach themselves by a mental necessity to the one name of Victoria; and then the character of Victoria must be derived from her action in them all.

manifestation of God is adapted to enable him as a rational being to comprehend God; and that by this manifestation he can approximate the absolute truth, far beyond any attainment he could make by his own unaided conception.

That man can have no just idea of God who endeavors to compass the divine mind in a single thought. The bare idea of power and Godhead transfers the mind back from the third to the first dispensation, when the Almighty was known as God of Creation only; not as Jehovah, more perfectly revealed to Moses, in the second dispensation; nor as God in Christ, most perfectly revealed in the New Testament. After we have apprehended God as the Father Almighty, and conceived of him as truth and love in Christ, and as an everywhere-present life and power in the Spirit; after the soul has appreciated and appropriated, by faith, all that there is in Father, Son, and Holy Ghost, then only it has arisen to the best knowledge that a finite mind can gain of the character of the true God. Hence it is written, "Go teach all nations, baptizing them into the ONE *name* but *three persons*—the FATHER, the SON, the HOLY GHOST—and lo! I am with you always, even to the end of the dispensation."

The Christian alone who has faith in the Trinity, as revealed in the New Testament, obtains an adequate and vitalizing knowledge of God. *The God of one intuition or conception is an abstract nullity, devoid of all moral power over human character and human life.* The God of one intuition, with the superadded characteristics which man's folly or his philosophy always frames when he is devoid of faith in revelation, is more or less an erroneous and corrupting conception. Christianity alone enlightens the natural mind, guides the reason, and matures the conception of the divine character. Hence the idea of God, as conceived by such men as Mr. Parker, who reject revealed religion, is incongruous and foolish. The Christian alone rises by faith to a knowledge of the living and true God, clothed in his attributes of power, light, and love.

Shall we not, then, my dear sir, turn away from the hallucinations of the skeptics, and the moonshine rationalisms of the transcendentalists, and seek in the Scriptures the knowledge of God, "whom to know ARIGHT is life eternal."

Yours in defense of revealed, rational, and spiritually-efficacious Christianity,

LETTER VI.

DEPRAVITY.

MY DEAR SIR :—

The doctrine of human depravity is rejected contemptuously by the skeptics of our day ; and with these there are many good and thoughtful men who misapprehend its import, and hence doubt of its truth. This latter class is led into doubt upon this subject about as much by the overstrained definition of some orthodox preachers, as they are by the same fault on the part of those who oppose Christianity as a system of revealed religion.

There is a basis in human reason and experience, as well as in revelation, for this doctrine ; and neither the misstatements of the friends of Christianity, nor the *mal*-statements of its enemies, can invalidate the facts and reasons upon which the doctrine rests.

The statement that men are by nature averse to all good, and as evil as it is possible for them to be, is not true to the common sense of men, nor in the common use of language. Such expressions may be explained into accordance with the Scriptures, but it is far better to avoid the extreme expression to which every denomination (from the very nature of selfishness) is prone to carry *its own* distinguishing tenets, and present the Christian doctrines in such phraseology as falls clearly within the import of the facts and texts upon which they are grounded.

While, therefore, there may be some apology for misapprehension on this subject, there can be no good apology for such mal-statement as that of Mr. Parker to which we have already alluded, viz., "The popular religion is hostile to man; tells us he is an outcast; not a child of God, *but a spurious issue of the devil.*"

The most trustworthy writers on this subject always state the question in its connections, and with the limitations which experience and the Bible require. Dr. Chalmers, in speaking of those who are unregenerated, says: "The principle upon which you may have acted may be respectable and honorable and amiable. We are not disputing all this. We are only saying that it is not the love of God. And should we hear any one of you assert that I have nothing to reproach myself with, and that I give every body their own, and that I possess a fair character in society, and have done nothing to forfeit it; and that I have my share of generosity and honor, of tenderness and civility: our only reply is, that this may be very true; you may have a very large share of these and of other estimable principles, but along with the possession of these many things, you may lack one thing, and that one thing may be the love of God. An enlightened discerner of the heart may look into you and say with our Saviour, 'I know you that ye have not the love of God in you.'"

We will give another extract from a writer generally accepted among evangelical Christians—one of the most clear-minded and pure-hearted men of his age. These extracts are given at length, in order that you may consider this subject unbiased by the opinion that the views which we shall present do not apply to the subject as generally received by enlightened Christians.

We do not, as we have already said, present our views as an exposition of the symbols of any one denomination—some of the creeds were wrought out by good men in a darker age than the present. We write to show that the doctrine of human depravity, as revealed in the Scriptures and expounded by men of spiritual apprehension, accords with reason and with human experience.

Dr. Dwight says: "*The human character is not depraved to the full extent of the human powers.* It has been said, neither unfrequently nor by men void of understanding, that man is as depraved a being as his faculties will permit him to be; but this has been said without consideration and without truth. Neither Scripture nor experience warrant the assertion. 'Wicked men and deceivers,' it is declared, 'wax worse and worse, deceiving and being deceived.' During the first half of human life this may, perhaps, be explained by the growth of the faculties, but during a considerable period preceding its termination it can not thus be explained, for the faculties decay while the depravity still increases." "The young man who came to Christ to know what good thing he should do to inherit eternal life, was certainly less depraved than his talents would have permitted him to be.

"Like him, we see daily many men who neither are nor profess to be Christians, and who, instead of being wicked to a degree commensurate with their faculties, go through life in the exercise of dispositions so sincere, just, and amiable, and in the performance of actions so upright and beneficent, as to secure a high degree of respect and affection from ourselves, and from all with whom they are connected. It certainly can not be said that such men are as sinful as many others possessed of powers far inferior, much less that they are as sinful as they can be. Those who make the assertion against which I am contending, will find themselves, if they will examine, rarely believing that their wives and children, though not Christians, are fiends."

Again, Dr. Dwight says: "Some of the natural human characteristics are amiable. Such are natural affection; the simplicity and sweetness of disposition in children, often found also in persons of adult years; compassion, generosity, modesty, and what is sometimes called *natural conscientiousness*, that is, a fixed and strong sense of the importance of doing that which is right. These characteristics appear to have adorned the young man whom I have already mentioned. We know that they are amiable, because we are informed that '*Jesus, beholding him, loved him.*' In the same manner we, and all others who are not abandoned, love them always and irresistibly, whenever they are presented to our view. They all, also, are required, and exist in every Christian, enhancing his holiness and rendering him a better man. Without them it is not easy to perceive how the Christian character could exist. Accordingly, Saint Paul exhibits those who are destitute of these attributes as being literally profligates."

If, then, the doctrine of human depravity, as expounded by the accepted teachers of the orthodox faith, does not affirm that man's faculties are wholly depraved; if it be a manifest and indubitable fact that men may possess by nature many excellent and amiable qualities for which we ought to love them; what then is the scriptural, rational, and experimental import of the doctrine of human depravity, and in what sense are all men depraved?

It is affirmed in the Scriptures, and Mr. Parker adopts the principle as a tenet of absolute religion, that man shall love God with all his heart, and his neighbor as himself. Of the obligation of this requirement there can be no doubt. God is the supreme being, and the best being, and, therefore, of right demands supreme love. The interests of other men are as valuable to them as our interests are to us; hence they should be regarded equally with our own. This is the moral law of the universe. To this all agree. Now, the question is not whether some men have not by nature many good qualities, nor whether any man is as bad as he could be? But the question is, *whether men do by nature love and obey God? whether they are by nature conformed or unconformed to the moral law of God?*

The question, when fairly stated, is a very plain one; and the man who doubts of human depravity in the light of a true statement, can have but little apprehension either of God's character or of his own. If men loved and obeyed the true God by nature, they would have to make an effort *not* to love and obey him. Every body knows that the reverse of this is true, and that the effort is on the other side of the question. But while argument may not make a palpable experience more plain to Christians, it may promote right conviction with those who are not. Let us, then, look first at the testimony of universal consciousness.

I need not recite to you those passages from the ancient classics with which you are more familiar than I am myself. Epictetus, speaking of the consciousness of every natural mind in which the moral sense is not obliterated, says, almost in the words of Paul, or rather Paul says, almost in his words, "He that sins does not what he would, but what he would not, that he does." In accordance with this speak all the worthy ancients who have given us their self-consciousness on moral subjects.

Take again the testimony of universal history. It can not be doubted that humanity has always been found by the light of history and revelation in a corrupted moral state. We mean, distinctly, in a state entirely destitute of supreme love to God as a holy sovereign, and to men as brothers. That civilization made progress in some old nations—that intellectual light and a perception of moral truths were in some minds clear and strong, is granted; but the knowledge of God, the disposition to love men as brethren, and a prevalent regard for moral purity, is *not the natural state* of man. The fact is striking as it is indubitable, that the most enlightened nations, as they increased in years, have invariably, without the aid of revelation, become more corrupt. And as they added years, they added evil to their national life. (Vide Phil. Plan Sal., ch. i.) And even now, in lands professing to receive the religion of Christ, and among those who recognize the obligation to love God as the common Father, and all men as brethren—even in Christendom, notwithstanding an assent to right principles, war and lust, pride and self-seeking, are the rule, and obedience to the recognized moral law of love is the exception.

Leaving the universal law of love out of the question, which is the recognized standard of duty, and to which man would be conformed if he, by nature, knew and obeyed the true God—even setting this aside, it is true that men have in all ages been conscious of being unconformed *to their own knowledge* of duty. This is evidenced by the fact, that the human consciousness of sin in all time (until Christ's sacrifice) has been evinced by the sacrifice of victims, human and bestial, as expiatory or propitiatory offerings, to procure reconciliation with God.

This testimony of universal consciousness, universal history, and universal conduct, can not go for nothing. To make a light thing of the deepest and most solemnly-expressed convictions of human nature, is to be untrue to humanity as it is. The human consciousness cries out for reconciliation with God. The man who answers that it needs none, is as injurious to the soul as a physician would be to the body, who, in a dangerous malady, should give opiates, and let the disease take its course.

But in view of Mr. Parker's own theories, how

can he avoid admitting the total depravity of human nature? Indeed, it is true that he, in statement, apparently unconscious that almost his whole book is in contradiction to this, utters words affirming the depravity of humanity and the necessity of Christ's death. He says (p. 467), "The history of society is summed up in a word—*Cain killed Abel.* That of real Christianity also in a word—*Christ died for his brothers.*"

The direct inference from Mr. Parker's philosophy goes likewise to establish the opposite of what he believes. If man has by intuition, or in some other way, a "true idea of God, which is the same in all men," then it follows as a fact corroborated by all history, that man must have propensities so totally depraved that they lead him to reject the true knowledge of the divine, and plunge into darkness and evil, notwithstanding the counter influence of Mr. Parker's absolute religion. If this be not an evidence of depravity, we would humbly inquire what can be evidence in the case?

Perhaps Mr. Parker would refer us to the conception which he says man gets from nature, and then tell us that the conception obscures the intuition. Then, two things follow—first, that all nature is depraved from which man gets the obscuring conception; and, second, that God has given man a true idea of himself, which is not strong enough to resist the depraving power of depraved nature. Yet Mr. Parker affirms "the popular doctrine of depravity" to be a "*No-fact.*"

But let us turn from the "variations" found in the "Discourses of Religion," and look at the appeal which may be made to each individual's consciousness in behalf of the doctrine of depravity.

Men will acknowledge that they do not live up to the amount of their knowledge—that they do not live up to their ability—that they do not live up to their conscience. Now, what is the reason of this? Who will answer? The brute lives up to the best instincts of his nature. The brute conforms by nature to the laws of his highest life and happiness. Why is not man thus conformed to the moral law of love? Why does he not by nature live a life like Christ? Let the reader frankly acknowledge that it is because the current of the human will runs in another direction. Hence it is the experience of every living man who seeks conformity to the will of God, that he must *struggle against* the inertia and earthly and selfish propensions of his natural mind. And it is likewise, as we believe, an experience, that divine aid alone enables the soul to rise above the natural into the spiritual life.

We repeat, if there be any thing plain in the Scriptures, it is the struggle or spiritual warfare that is necessary to *attain* and MAINTAIN conformity to the will of God as manifested in Christ. If there be any thing true in *Christian experience* it is this same warfare—a warfare which reaches a conscious and joyful triumph only by faith in Christ, as a present divine Saviour. If men by nature be not out of conformity with the law of God, then the whole tenor of the New Testament and all Christian experience are together false, because the one affirms what the other realizes.

But it is not possible to lead any man who has ever seriously endeavored to be like Christ, to doubt that by nature his will "is alienated from the life of God." *Transcendentalism may lead men of no Christian purpose to doubt, but it can do no more.* The man who permits his boat to float upon the current of Lake Superior will move downward *without an effort* to the more rapid current of the Niagara river. He can not be conscious of any effort, because he makes none. It requires no effort to float with the current. But if a man will save himself from going over the falls, he must turn his boat against the stream, and his labors will grow light, and his hope and peace will increase, as he escapes the dangerous current, and sees on the farthermost verge of the lake the light-house of the homeward-bound. So the Christian who has struggled against the natural current of the will, finds peace as he overcomes, and rejoices as the light grows brighter which shines out from the "light-house in the sky."

The teachings of the Scriptures on this subject not only accord with experience, but they contain a profound philosophy, which will, by some future writer, be developed in a more satisfactory manner than it is at present. Allow me, in conclusion, an allusion to this philosophy.

Adam, the origin of our transmitted humanity, is said to have been a "living soul." Christ, the source of our *spiritual* and *eternal life*, is "a quickening Spirit." We inherit from Adam an earthly nature, whose appetites, motives, aspirations, are limited to the earth. This is, in the language of the New Testament, "the natural mind," "the old man," "the flesh." The first birth is natural, and gives to man only earthly and selfish instincts and aspirations. Man by nature may be an amiable and excellent earthly being, or he may be a morally deformed and despicable one; but still he is "of the earth earthy," and, as Jesus affirmed, "the love of God is not in him." He is "alive" to earthly and selfish motives and objects; but he is "dead unto God;" he does not feel and move in view of what God is, nor in view of what he has commanded. In his mind *his own will*, not the will of God, is supreme; and he resists subjection to the will of God as much as an animal (*fere naturæ*), *wild by nature*, resists subjection to the will of man. The divine Teacher affirmed the foundational truth on this subject when he said, "That which is born of the flesh is flesh, that which is born of the Spirit is spirit."

Christ is a "life-giving Spirit;" and the new spiritual life which proceeds from him is superinduced upon an animal or earthly nature. Christians are twice born—first by nature—again by Spirit. By the second birth, the soul that was spiritually dead before, begins to live and move in view of God's character, will, and manifested benevolence in Christ. By the first birth every man has the mental and fleshly nature of Adam; by the second birth every believer has in him the spiritual lineaments of Christ. This new divine nature is developed out of the old earthly nature, or superinduced upon it. As the chrysalis has the lineaments of the butterfly within it, while yet it retains the body, and, to some extent, the instincts of the caterpillar, so the Christian has the spiritual lineaments of Christ formed in his soul while yet he retains the earthly nature of his earthly progenitor. In the resurrection the spiritual soul, disenthralled from its Adamic corporeity, will assimilate to itself, by divine power, a body of a spiritual nature, adapted to the propensions of its new spiritual life, "fashioned like unto Christ's glorious body." Hence, the "image of Christ formed in the soul" *here*, is the *only "hope of glory" hereafter.*

The spiritual and the earthly nature—the one being superinduced upon the other—are antagonistic the one to the other. It is reasonable to suppose that, as in the lipodeptera, the rudiments of the winged insect prevail against the worm from which it is developed, the antagonistic efforts of the two opposing instincts are *felt*, and the one prevails over the other *with a struggle;* so, in the case of those who are "born of the Spirit," "the flesh lusteth against the Spirit, and the Spirit against the flesh, and these are contrary the one to the other."

When a man is born again, the two natures are

distinctly marked by the diverse aliment upon which they live. The natural mind lives on natural aliment, and seeks its highest good on earth. The spiritual mind grows and develops itself by truth. The new nature draws its life from Christ. The conscience, the affections, and the will, live and move in view of God in Christ. God becomes the spiritual Father of the spiritual soul, and the "new-created" is a son. Truth is eternal—Christ is eternal. Hence, the soul which lives on this aliment has eternal life. Jesus said, "*I am the bread of life, of which if a man eat he shall never die, but shall have everlasting life.*" The natural man "liveth by bread alone," but the Christian liveth "by every word that proceedeth out of the mouth of God."

In the light of this philosophy, which is discriminatingly true to the Scriptures, we may see the reason and the necessity of the doctrine of the divine Spirit. The glory of the gospel is in its power, offered at this point, to transform the human soul from the habitudes of an earthly to that of a spiritual life. A nature can not transform itself. One species can not produce another. The instincts of the earthly nature can not turn against themselves. The germ of the new nature must be "begotten" in order to prevail against the old. When the new nature is begotten, the old nature becomes as a body of death, until the new rises above it, and brings it into subserviency.

The Scriptures exhibit this subject more distinctly than I am able to do. I will close this long letter with a quotation, and some inferences from it.

The apostle, in his letter to the Romans, says: "There is, therefore, now no condemnation to them which are in Christ Jesus, who walk not after the flesh, but after the Spirit; for the law of the Spirit of Life in Christ Jesus hath made me free from the law of sin and death. For what the law could not do in that it was weak through the flesh [or because of the earthly nature], God sending his own Son in the likeness of sinful flesh, and for sin [as a sacrifice for sin], condemned sin in the flesh, that the righteousness of the law may be fulfilled in us, who walk, not after the flesh but after the Spirit [i. e. not after the old nature, but the new]. For they who have only the earthly nature—'are earthly'—do interest themselves only in the things of the earth; and they that have the spiritual nature are interested in the things of the Spirit. For to be carnally-minded is death. [Those who are governed only by earthly and selfish motives and aims are spiritually dead.] But to be spiritually-minded *is life and peace.* For the carnal mind is enmity against God. It is not subject to his law, neither indeed can be. So then, they that are in the flesh [or natural state] can not please God.

"*But if the Spirit of him that raised up Jesus Christ from the dead dwell in you, he that raised up Christ from the dead shall also quicken your mortal bodies by his Spirit that dwelleth in you.*"

Look a moment at one or two of the points in this passage.

The law can give knowledge of duty, but it can not beget life. It can show us the evil, but it can not beget the disposition to overcome the evil. It is not knowledge that men want, but strength to do what they know. The man is a fool who supposes that light is love. The law requires love, but it can not beget it. Every thing begets its kind. Love only can beget love. Hence, Christ crucified in the humanity as a sacrifice for sin, is such an exhibition of love that it begets love in believers. Faith accomplishes "what the law could not do." Love is life. "Love is the fulfilling of the law," and hence "the law of God is fulfilled in us who walk not after the flesh, but after the Spirit." Men by nature are morally "dead already," and have no "eternal life" unless born again by the Spirit of Holiness in Christ Jesus.

In the Christian are the rudiments of a new species—a new and higher type of the rational order of humanity. His new life is by divine interposition, but received in accordance with his own voluntary powers—begotten by truth and cherished by love. The spiritual germ is implanted and developed here until it attains the resurrection state—i. e. overcomes the habitudes of its earthly body—then, in the resurrection, a spiritual body adapted to its propensions is given to it. "To every seed its own [adapted] body." Christ is the head and the type of the new creation (shall we say of the new species?). Let us rejoice, my friend. The process now developing in Christian minds on the earth, will reach, in body and spirit, a glorious consummation in the resurrection of the just.

Yours, in the hope that we shall awake in his likeness,

LETTER VII.

RECONCILIATION, OR AT-ONE-MENT.

MY DEAR SIR :—

You know that the Christian doctrine of *atonement* is held confidingly by the evangelical churches; but, as we have seen, this doctrine is determinedly rejected by Mr. Parker and other skeptics, as it is likewise by a portion of those calling themselves Unitarians.

It should be stated at the outset that the subject of sacrifice has its essential relations with the moral nature of man—the conscience, the affections, the will, rather than with the intellect. The love-power of sacrifice when appropriated by faith—its relations to man's moral nature, and to God's moral government—is too profound to be fully developed by mere logical elucidation. The sacrifice of Christ is a manifestation of power and love transferred by faith to the consciousness of the believer. The skeptic can not know this. Hence the main evidence is absent in his case. But there are adaptations of the atonement to imperfect humanity—there are grounds of its necessity in moral government, which may be seen by the reason; and seeing these, a reason that is reverent will accept the aid of faith which gives us the substance of what the reason had given us distinct indications.

We inquire, then, is there any thing in the nature of man which is met only by the sacrifice of Christ, offered not for himself, but for those who will accept its mercy by faith?

It can not be doubted that there is in man a consciousness of sin, or of something else (call it what you will) that leads him to feel the want of a sacrifice—or rather that leads him to sacrifice as a means of reconciliation with God. Since the world began man has had something in his soul that has led him to offer sacrifice. We inquire neither for the reason of the fact, nor for the form of the fact, but for the fact itself. Men may call the fact propitiation, expiation, substitution—by any or all these names, still the thing sought by the soul is plain:—*It is peace with God, a mitigation of the consciousness of sin, reconciliation, at-one-ment.* Superstitious usages have been connected with sacrifice, and priestcraft has turned the offering of the sin-oppressed soul to a selfish account; but the perversion of the fact does not ignore the existence of the sense of want which has produced in all ages and among all nations, the various phenomena of sacrifices.

The ultimate truth in the case, then, is, that there is something in the human soul that leads it to seek peace with God by sacrifice. The form may be varied never so much. Some may inflict torture upon themselves; some part with, as an offering, what they deem most precious, even a son or a daughter; some make a pilgrimage; some offer the first-fruits of grain or of cattle. Whatever the form, the phenomena are all produced by the one want of the sin-conscious soul—a desire of peace, or at-one-ment with God.

The want of atonement felt in the soul is as universal as the sense of sin. Man, therefore, as a being, naturally seeks reconciliation by sacrifice, because his reason, as well as his moral sense, teaches him that sin alienates and separates from God.

In this connection notice an important fact—a fact which is evidence not only of the fallen and darkened state of the human mind, but likewise of the necessity of revelation, especially of the revelation of the mercy of God by sacrifice. While the sense of sin, which is universal, produces in men the sense of want which demands a propitiation, yet to offer self, or any object we can call our own, produces selfishness and pride in the soul instead of benevolence, gratitude, and humility. We feel the want of a sacrifice, but nothing we possess produces the effect necessary in order to peace of conscience and purity of heart. The man who goes upon a pilgrimage to Mecca, or to any other shrine, especially if he has walked on his knees a part of the way, *returns to his home a censorious and self-righteous spirit*, his self-sacrifice having led him away from humility, and rendered gratitude impossible. *He can not be grateful to God for a salvation which he himself has worked out for himself.* So with the devotee who tortures himself. So in the case of those who give, as a propitiation, money or cattle. The effect necessarily connected with sacrifice, when that sacrifice is made *by* SELF *for* SELF, is the opposite of that which the sacrifice of Christ for the sinner is adapted to produce. The one produces self-righteousness and self-dependence—the other gratitude and dependence on God.*

This then is the actual condition of man in his

* It is a singular fact that Mr. Parker makes out, that a "sense of dependence" is the ultimate idea in religion (p. 18), and yet discards the doctrine which alone produces a sense of dependence.

natural state. He has a sense of sin, and the accompanying sense of sacrifice, but the selfish sacrifices to which his natural want leads, produce evil and not good in the soul. Instead of rendering a man humble and grateful, the sacrifices prompted by the natural want, and offered by self for self, produce pride and impiety. It has done so since the beginning of the world, and would have continued to do so until the end of the world, if divine revelation and a divine sacrifice had not revealed Christ crucified, which rescues the soul from selfish sacrificing. Skeptics can not deny these facts. If they reject the gospel solution of them, we defy them to furnish any other that does not impugn either the justice or the mercy of God; and thus involve the difficulty in deeper darkness, rather than resolve it by light and love revealed in "the Lamb slain from the foundation of the world," to be "testified to all in due time."

In what way, then, could the natural want of propitiation be met, and the soul receive spiritual good by the sacrifice?

We probably have anticipated the answer to this question. But let us look at one or two particulars. In the first place, it is necessary, in order to the formation of a benevolent character, that the motive of our action be out of self. What I do for another makes me more benevolent. What I do from selfish motives makes me more selfish. Now the man who has faith in Christ's love-sacrifice for us, is redeemed from a selfish motive. He labors for Christ's sake. Christ's sacrifice moves him. He is God-moved, not self-moved. Christ becomes motive both in the heart and in the will. Faith produces gratitude and good works, but works can never produce faith.

The sacrifice of Christ then is a necessary part of the moral system which includes man as a sinner. Without it the natural sense of sin and dependence works injury to the human soul. With it the sense of sin in believers is canceled by a sense of reconciliation, and reason and conscience find rest by trust in the divine sacrifice. A sense of dependence, now, places the soul in its true position. It depends not on itself, but on the love of God manifested in Christ's sacrifice. And every time we pray in his name the sense of dependence and gratitude is renewed in the mind.

The introductory dispensation of Moses produced, so far as an initiatory process of types and figures could produce, the salutary ideas which are produced under the Christian dispensation by the sacrifice of Christ.

The faith and ritual of the Mosaic institution was such, that the sacrifice offered was not deemed the property of the individual, but as belonging to the Lord (Exodus, xiii. 11–16). The Lord permitted the redemption by sacrifice of the first-born, which belonged to him by the most solemn covenant. The ceremonial was such that it was to the mind of the Jew the Lord's sacrifice, while yet it was permitted to be offered for a sin or a peace-offering. Thus the idea of *own*ership in the offering was destroyed by the plan of the Mosaic economy; hence, the concomitant idea of pride and self-righteousness could not follow the offering. The fee of the sacrifice was in Jehovah, not in the sinner who offered it.

But as a sense of sin would again arise by renewed transgression or omission of known duty, hence a succession of sacrifices was the burden of the old law. These sacrifices, says the apostle, could not make the comers thereunto perfect. The renewed sense of sin required a renewed sacrifice. The thing needed to meet the want was one sacrifice that could be pleaded perpetually, which would thus make the comers perfect, and supersede forever the offering of sacrifices by the people of God. Hence the whole system is fulfilled in the sacrifice of Christ. He is "the end of the law [of sacrifice] to every one that believeth." "Nor yet (Heb. ix. 25) that he should offer himself often, as the high priest entereth into the holy place every year with the blood of others;" "but now *once* in the end of the dispensation hath he appeared to put away sin by the sacrifice of himself." Hence, "the blood of Christ who *by the eternal Spirit* offered himself without spot unto God, *will purge your consciences from dead works to serve the living God.*"

It is not necessary to inquire, as some have done, whether in the darkness of the age, the divine Father adapted the sacrifices which the natural want had produced, and which were then existing, to the end of initiating the one sacrifice offered by the eternal Spirit, which would more perfectly purify the conscience and heart, and produce obedience by a right motive. It is enough to know the fact that the sacrifice of Christ does purify the heart—speaks peace to the conscience—redeems the soul from selfish or dead works—and produces works of love in those who are servants of the living God.

There is another aspect of the atonement which is

frequently brought to view in the Scriptures, and which many consider the foundation of its necessity.

Man has an innate sense of justice and right. This is a distinguishing attribute of his moral nature. A sense of responsibility for all moral action of which conscience takes cognizance is based upon it. A sense of the evil and desert of sin arises, in a great measure, from the sense of justice, which is in conflict with sin. Law is the development of justice, as benevolence is the development of love. Love often develops itself in acts which are superior to law, because they are acts of self-denial which the law or justice does not demand. But laws are the immutable rules of the creation, physical and moral; and mercy is never rightly exercised except it be to bring the ignorant and erring back to light and law. Justice, then, underlies mercy, and mercy is exercised in maintainance of the principles of eternal justice. Mercy rises above the law only to bring back the transgressor into conformity to law.

Now, God having given to man this foundational sense of justice, would not violate it by atonement or in any other way. Beside, God himself possesses the attribute of justice, and his moral government, even in the administration of mercy, must be based upon it.

The principle of justice, then, which develops itself in law can not be sacrificed to the power of mercy which develops itself in benevolence; notwithstanding benevolence often rises above the requirements of law. Nor can the one produce the effects which the other does in the human mind. Gratitude can not be exercised fully for an action in others which the law requires of them. We must see in the act something of the mercy which produces acts of *personal self-denial for us*, before gratitude flows spontaneously. But the being who, while he maintains the principles of justice, exercises mercy by acts of self-denial which the law does not require, commends himself both to the conscience and the affections of moral beings, and begets in all right minds not only a sense of respect and benevolence, but at the same time a sense of grateful love for the benefactor.

There are many who seem to have no right sense of the principles of justice and mercy as they relate to moral government. This state of mind is born of ignorance and sin. God is not only the Father, especially of those who are "born of the Spirit," but he is the ruler and judge of men. A father may pardon a son for an offense against himself; but if he is a magistrate, and that son commits the same offense against the public law, he can not pardon him without forfeiting his character as a ruler, or impairing the sense of justice in the public mind.

If the sense of justice is *of* God and *in* God, he will maintain it in moral government. The best men have the strongest sense of justice.

A proclamation of pardon on repentance would render repentance a selfish act, or make it impossible.

"God is love," and therefore in governing the world he would exercise benevolence; but benevolence would be exercised in such a manner as to maintain the sense of justice, which is the basis of moral government.

We desire not only to elucidate this subject, but to produce positive conviction in relation to it. Instead of reproducing the same thought, allow me to refer you to the chapters on law and atonement in "God Revealed in Creation and in Christ," beginning with the second book, and thence onward to the 198th page.*

* It was my intention, in printing these Letters, to introduce as notes, or as an appendix, several quotations from my previous works ("The Philosophy of the Plan of Salvation," and "God Revealed," etc.), but the excellent publishers of these works, Messrs. Gould & Lincoln, of Boston, were not willing that such large extracts should be made from books, the copyright of which is owned by themselves.

I have no doubt their views of the matter are proper; hence I

I commend most heartily the whole subject of *law* and *atonement*, in the beginning of the Second Book, to your attention (I have marked the emphatic passages in the volume expressed to you). Please read them with the conviction in mind, that in order to maintain the principle of justice in the minds of intelligent beings, God must develop and maintain this principle in his own moral government. And in connection with this, keep in mind that benevolence, which is above law, can be properly exercised only to bring back transgressors to obedience to law. As law is the only foundation of order in the moral universe, and of safety and happiness to the creature, benevolence can be exercised in no way that is congruous with the system, except in the pardon and restoration of offenders.

Notice, with me, an outline of the principles upon which this conclusion is predicated.

The universe, physical and moral, is founded in

have quoted but little of the passages to which I had referred my respondent. In one or two cases in which the thought is necessary to the completeness of my argument, I have reproduced my own thought in other forms. To this I think there can be no objection, as those able writers, *Rev. Dr. Hopkins*, in his Lowell Lectures, and *Dr. Berg*, in his Discussion with Barker, have reproduced, in their own words, some of the most valuable thought in my first volume. It is perhaps due to myself to say that my volume was published some time before the appearance of those works.

law and governed by law. In obedience to law there is safety and happiness. Whatever transgresses law has taken the first step in the road to ruin. Law knows, and can know, no pardon. As life in any case is impossible without obedience to law, pardon while the transgressor is not restored would be a nullity and an absurdity.

Whatever departs from law secures derangement in the beginning and death in the end; and in addition to its own aberration, produces derangement in other things. If an orb were to leave its sphere, it would not only rush to destruction, but it would cross other orbits, and dash itself against other bodies. In such an event the system would be destroyed unless the deranged body could be drawn back before the final destruction, and at the same time a re-adjustment be made of the derangement which it had caused in the system. When any thing departs from the rule of law, it has no power to recover itself or to rectify the error. In the physical universe the slightest departure would unbalance the attractive forces, and the tendency would be to swifter departure. The very laws which preserve from destruction every thing in obedience to them, hastens and compels the destruction of whatever departs from obedience.

So in the moral world; one sin tends to produce another. Sin weakens the moral forces which hold the soul to obedience. Like all other derangements, the tendency to sin augments itself by its own activity; hence, in the moral world, as in the physical, the import of the sentence is, "the soul that sinneth it shall die."

Moral transgression, likewise, not only puts the soul in the road to ruin, but it deranges other moral agents. One sinner causes sin in others. Sin begets sin. As the leprosy, which symbolized its influence in the camp of Israel, sin is contagious. It ruins one while it infects others.

"Law, then, is a necessity of things, and penalty is a necessity of law." Law is inexorable. Every transgression tends to the destruction of the subject; while the subject, by the transgression, is put without the pale of safety, and rendered incapable, in himself, of returning or of compensating for his transgression.

This inviolability of moral law finds a sanction in the reason and conscience of men. The moral law is an expression of the will of God. He could not, therefore, permit sin without permitting a violation of his own will, which would be absurd. Beside, if God is holy he ought not to make a law which would permit sin. No man will say that God ought to make a law that would allow a single transgression. Now, if the reason and conscience that God has given men say, and sanction the saying, that God ought not to permit sin, who dare rebel against his moral nature, and say that *he has* done so? Reason affirms, conscience sanctions, and the moral law reveals the same penalty that is written against the transgressor of every other law of the universe—*The transgressing subject shall die.*

Now, then, man is a sinner. In gospel-enlightened lands, he has not lived up to his knowledge of good; nor up to the demands of conscience; nor up to the amount of his ability. He is a transgressor of the moral law of God, and the penalty of that law—" dying thou shalt die"—is against him. His moral nature is deranged, and tending to the second death.

How, now, shall man be restored and pardoned? How shall the evil propension be regenerated, and the evil he has occasioned in others be balanced and compensated for? Is there any method by which, without impairing the sense of justice, benevolence, which is above law, may restore the transgressor to obedience, and arrest the evils which his sin has occasioned in other minds? This is the problem of the atonement. Let us see.

There are, in the physical universe and in physical and instinctive law, compensations which are placed over against each other; and thus the inequalities of the various systems of law are met and balanced. These compensations or adjustments are made by the Creator; and they become at once the evidences of his wisdom and goodness.

Are there likewise deviations and compensations in the moral universe? We can answer only for ourselves, as moral beings, and as we are related to the moral law.

1. The moral law, which requires supreme love to God and impartial love to man, is the rule of reason and righteousness; and being the will of God, it is the obligatory law for all intelligent and moral beings. From this statement I presume there will be no dissent. Certainly none by yourself.

2. Now, accepting the law as the rule of life, it is admitted that man falls below its requirements—that, judged by the law, he is condemned as a transgressor. He is guilty in view of his own conscience, knowledge, and ability. He is likewise guilty in nature (or, if you prefer it, in character),

not having the disposition to fulfill his duties according to the example of Christ. The penalties of the law are therefore against him, and he can neither pardon himself nor beget that love in himself which is the fulfilling of the law.

3. The law, then, is the rule of life. Man is below its requirements, and therefore liable to destruction as the penalty of transgression. He is without love to God—dead already, and tending to the "second death." Now, is there any compensation in the moral universe for this aberration of man from the sphere of law? Is there a recuperative principle in the moral as there is in the physical system of things?—a redeeming power adapted to the nature of the case?

The thing required in order to moral compensation is that *some being, united in the same system with man, should possess a moral worth rising above law in the same degree that man falls below it.* Now, we postulate that Jesus Christ, by his sacrifice, meets this condition in the equation. The law can not demand the sacrifice of the innocent for the guilty. Its requirement can rise no higher than perfect obedience. The death of Christ, therefore, was above law; and if it tended to honor the law by restoring transgressors to obedience, it accomplished on one side an actual balance against what was deficient on the other side.

The question, then, of vital interest is, *does the super-merit of Christ, which is above law, practically counterwork the demerit of man, which is below law?* Now, we affirm that this result is actually and practically accomplished in every one that believes in the divine sacrifice of the Redeemer.

"Love is the fulfilling of the law." Christ's sacrifice was a love-sacrifice—a sacrifice produced by divine love. The law required obedience, but could not produce it. It required love, but could not beget love. The sacrifice of Christ is a revealment of divine love, and hence—as every thing begets its kind—by the love of God manifest in Christ, love for God in Christ is begotten in believers. Now, "if men love God, they will keep his commandments." Hence the disposition to obedience is restored in the soul of every one who believes in Christ. Thus the current of death which originated in Adam is met and counteracted by the *life*-current which originated in Christ. One was made a "living soul," that is, an earthly being—the other is a "quickening," that is, *life-giving Spirit.*

Now, you know that faith in Christ disposes men

to love and obey him. You know more than this. You know that in the case of your own relatives, it produces peaceful obedience in the soul—it casts out sin—it works by love, and purifies the heart.

What then, is the thing which constitutes the merit and power of the divine sacrifice? We answer, *its merit is in its love, which is above law.* Its personal suffering endured for others. This fact likewise constitutes its power. I can not love with the love of gratitude one who does no more for me than the law requires him to do. But when love transcends law, and one rescues me by a sacrifice of himself, a sacrifice which love prompted, but which law did not require, then my heart, and the heart of every believer responds by grateful love to the Redeemer. Thus "faith works by love," and love works by obedience.

The merit, then, is found in the sacrifice of Christ, which, as an expression of divine love, restores the transgressor and procures pardon by balancing his demerit in the sight of the law. By this *merit* the sinner can be pardoned, while by its *power* he is redeemed from sin, and restored to obedience.

Thus law and love are the complement of each other in the divine government; and Christ came in our humanity "to give himself a ransom for many, that whosoever believeth might not perish but have eternal life."

Yours, for a life-giving faith.

LETTER VIII.

ON FUTURE RETRIBUTION.

My Dear Sir:—

You have not, I presume, any distinct impression of the views of Mr. Parker on the subject of *future retribution.* He frequently refers to the subject, but does not often announce his own opinions. There are passages, however, in which he speaks distinctly. Such an one occurs on page 438: "The woes of sin are its antidote. Suffering comes from wrong-doing, as well-being from virtue. If there be suffering in the next world, it is, as in this, but the medicine of the sickly soul."

This is plain. Mr. Parker adopts the opinions of those who are called Universalists on the subject of future retribution. He is wiser than those generally are who think with him. He affirms without argument. Others argue, and in their argument reason sees the fallacy.

We can not but doubt of the sincerity of men who profess to find their religion in the Bible, and yet tell us they believe in no future punishment. The Bible can not be interpreted to favor such views except by subterfuge and perversion on the part of the interpreter. Mr. Parker, therefore, seldom refers to the Bible on this subject. There is at least frankness in the audacity of the skeptic who sets his own reason above the reason of the Bible, and rejects or modifies it when it does not accord with his own conceptions. But to assume that the Bible is in agreement with the doctrine of no future punishment, is a *subtlety* that "perverts the right ways of the Lord," and indicates dishonesty in the interpreter.

We shall give the more attention to this subject, because it is one of vital interest to all persons who enjoy the light of the gospel. It has to do with the motives which deter men from sin. We do not say that Christians act in view of future retribution. Love deters the Christian from sin. For them there is no evil in the future. But for the unthankful and disobedient—for those who abuse the divine mercy and harden themselves in selfishness—there *is* evil in the future; and repentance with such is impossible so long as they believe there is no future punishment. Convince an impenitent man that sin will not exclude him from future happiness—that all the evil he will experience is present inconvenience or compunction of conscience—and with such convictions, repentance toward God and faith in our Lord Jesus Christ are out of the question. Every wicked man is willing to take the sin with its present evil; and as for the figment, that the consequences of sin will cure sin, or remove the cause of sinning, it is, as we shall see further on, contrary to both reason and the Scriptures.

An absurd argument is destroyed so soon as its absurdity is made apparent. The Universalist view of the future state, which Mr. Parker adopts, can be shown to be absurd both by reason and Scripture. We shall endeavor to make this apparent, and to reach, by our conclusion, the evil not only as it is maintained by Mr. Parker, but as it prevails in a wider sense.

You will notice that in this and succeeding chapters, and indeed in all I have written on this subject, I use the Scripture phrases, without discussing the questions at issue between denominations, in relation to *what will be the character of future punishment*—I make no effort to determine the mode of punishment, whether it be to sin and suffer forever, or whether the "second death" be the death of the soul. Archbishop Whately and others have discussed those points. We argue only the question at issue with Mr. Parker and those who, like him, believe in no future punishment; or, if there be any, that it is only disciplinary. We do not wish to occupy space with any other issue than the main one. The main question is not whether "God will destroy the soul and body of the wicked in hell?" or whether he will permit them to live sinning and suffering forever. The negative of the position that *all men will be saved*, is, that *all men will* NOT *be saved*. We believe this point is plain, whether we view it in the light of reason or of revelation. The other question concerning eternal sin and suffering, or the destruction of those unfitted for heaven, admits of discussion, and whichever way it may be settled by any one, the vital doctrines of the Scripture remain intact. In either case, the finally impenitent never enter the kingdom of the blessed.

My own opinion is, that while many expressions of the New Testament favor the doctrine that those unfitted for heaven will suffer the "second death" by the "destruction of both soul and body in hell," yet the specific expression of the Saviour in the 25th chapter of Matthew requires a different interpretation. I do not now see how any fair exegesis will give any other sense to this passage than the one which the great body of evangelical Christians have received, namely, that those who have rejected Christ and disobeyed his commands, will be doomed to "everlasting punishment," while the righteous will inherit "life eternal." The difficulty of construing this passage in accordance with the opinion that the "destruction of ungodly men" is the destruction of the soul, is given with distinctness and discrimination by Professor Post, in a recent article in the *New-Englander*.* We have extracted that part of this article which relates to the passage referred to.

In all discussions relating to this subject we use Scripture phrases. We shall prove that those who die unregenerated will "never see life." Whether they will be annihilated after the judgment, or sin and suffer forever, we leave for Mr. Parker and the Universalists to determine.

We are aware that the intensity and eternity of future misery have sometimes been urged with a spirit which indicated any thing else in the polemic beside a sense of the justice of God. Advantage has been taken of this by bad minds to create preju-

* See Appendix.

dice against evangelical piety, and to destroy in the minds of those who disobey the gospel the salutary impression that without repentance they will be "reserved unto the day of judgment to be punished."

Let us leave, then, whatever may be doubtful or difficult concerning the mere *form* of the doctrine of future punishment, and consider the main question. We affirm that neither Scripture nor reason teach the future salvation of those who die impenitent; but that they will "perish" in the "second death"—whatever that second death may be.

Notice, first, the absurdity of any effort which seeks to derive the doctrine of no future punishment from the Scriptures. By willful perversion, Universalism might be tortured out of Bunyan, or Baxter, or Edwards, much more readily than it can be out of the Bible. By the same artifice universal damnation may be proved—the one as readily as the other. Let us see.

Universal salvation proved by perverting the Scriptures.	*Universal damnation proved by perverting the Scriptures.*
1st John, i. 9. God is faithful and just to forgive us our sins: and to cleanse us from all unrighteousness.	Joshua, xxiv. 19. He is a holy God, he is a jealous God, he will not forgive your transgressions nor your sins.

Universal salvation proved by perverting the Scriptures.	*Universal damnation proved by perverting the Scriptures.*
Lam. iii. 31. For the Lord will not cast off forever.	1st Chron. xviii. 9. If thou seek him he will be found of thee; but if thou forsake him he will cast thee off forever.
All will be saved, because the Scriptures say—Mal. ii. 10, "Have we not all one father? Hath not one God created us?"	All will be damned, because the Scriptures say—Isaiah, xxvii. 11, He that made them will not have mercy on them; and he that formed them will show them no favor.
The world will be saved, because the Bible says, Christ gives eternal life to as many as the Father hath given him; and in another place it says, the Father hath put all things into his hands—so that the proof is clear that all will be saved in Christ.	The world will be damned, because the Bible says—They who have not the spirit of Christ are none of his; and in another place it says positively, the world can not receive the spirit of Christ—therefore it follows that the whole world must inevitably be damned.
All men will be saved, because the Bible teaches that Christ will reconcile all things unto himself—Col. i. 20—and says in another place that we "see not now all things reconciled," implying that all will be reconciled hereafter. Here is universal reconciliation and salvation plainly proved.	All men will be damned, because the Bible teaches, Jude 15, that the Lord cometh with ten thousand of his saints to execute judgment upon *all* (παντων all things); and if we do not see judgment executed upon all now, yet the passage says, the Lord cometh, or will come, to execute judgment on all things hereafter.

The words "forever," "everlasting," "forever and ever," occur frequently in the Scriptures, sometimes in connection with temporal, sometimes with spiritual subjects. An attempt has always been made by those who hold the views of Mr. Parker, to strip these words of their usual import, which is that of endless duration. Sometimes, as all know, they are applied to temporal things, when the common sense of the reader, as in all other similar cases, will limit them by the nature of the subject. "The everlasting hills" will stand while time lasts; God and the soul live when time dies. When these words are limited in signification, the limitation grows out of the nature of the subject. To this all agree; and this is all that is necessary to show the absurdity of the effort to destroy their import in connection with the future destiny of the wicked.

THE WORD "EVERLASTING" APPLIED TO EXPRESS THE DURATION OF THE

Happiness of the Righteous.	*Misery of the Wicked.*
Matth. xix. 29. Those that leave all to follow Christ shall "receive an hundred-fold, and shall inherit *everlasting* life."	2 Thess. i. 8, 9. The Lord Jesus shall be revealed from heaven, in flaming fire, taking vengeance on them that know not God, and obey not the gospel of our Lord Jesus Christ, *who shall be punished with* EVERLASTING *destruction from the presence of the Lord and the glory of his power.*
Luke, xviii. 30. They "shall receive manifold more in this present time, and in the world to come, life *everlasting.*"	Matth. xxv. 41. Depart from me, ye *cursed*, into *everlasting* fire, prepared for the devil and his angels.

Happiness of the Righteous.	*Misery of the Wicked.*
Romans, vi. 22. But now being made free from sin and become servants of God, ye have your fruit unto holiness, and the END, *everlasting life.*	Matth. xviii. 8. If thy hand or thy foot offend thee, cut them off and cast them from thee; it is better for thee to enter into life halt or maimed, rather than having two hands or two feet to be *cast into* EVERLASTING *fire.*
Dan. xii. 2. Many of them which sleep in the dust of the earth shall awake, *some to* EVERLASTING *life*, and some to shame and everlasting contempt.	Dan. xii. 2. Many of them which sleep in the dust of the earth shall awake, some to everlasting life, and some to *shame and* EVERLASTING *contempt.*
Matth. xxv. 46. These shall go away into everlasting punishment, but the *righteous into life* EVERLASTING.	Matth. xxv. 46. These shall go away into EVERLASTING *punishment*, but the righteous into life everlasting.

THE PHRASE "FOREVER AND EVER" AS APPLIED TO EXPRESS THE DURATION OF THE

Happiness of the Righteous.	*Misery of the Wicked.*
Dan. xii. 3. They that turn many to righteousness shall shine as stars *forever and ever.*	Rev. xiv. 11. The smoke of their torment ascendeth up *forever and ever*, and they have no rest day nor night.
Rev. xxii. 5. The Lord God giveth them light, and they shall reign *forever and ever.*	Rev. xx. 10. The devil, the beast, and the false prophet shall be tormented day and night *forever and ever.*

Mark, now. We do not argue from these tables that either the existence of punishment or of happiness is eternal. This is as clearly revealed as any words in the Hebrew or Greek language can reveal it; but this is not our argument. Our proposition is, that the destruction of the wicked will be as enduring as the happiness of the righteous, because both are supported by precisely the same proof. If Mr. Parker and his friends affirm that these words never mean eternal duration, then they get rid of everlasting punishment; but they likewise get rid of the everlasting God, and of the everlasting life of the righteous.

If they say that they sometimes mean eternal duration, and sometimes limited duration—that the duration is to be inferred from the nature of the subject to which they are applied; then the subject to which they are applied is the same in both cases, man—or the soul of man, or the body of man. Whatever they may choose to call the subject, there is no doubt but that it is the same in both cases.

If they reject both of these, and argue that the words "everlasting," and "eternal," and "forever," do not apply to the soul, but to the punishment or misery of the soul or body; then, on the other hand, the words do not apply to the soul of the righteous, but to the happiness or joy of the soul or body, and if misery is not eternal in its nature, then joy or happiness is not eternal in its nature.

Now, whatever these words mean in one case,

LETTER VIII.

ON FUTURE RETRIBUTION.

MY DEAR SIR:—

You have not, I presume, any distinct impression of the views of Mr. Parker on the subject of *future retribution.* He frequently refers to the subject, but does not often announce his own opinions. There are passages, however, in which he speaks distinctly. Such an one occurs on page 438: "The woes of sin are its antidote. Suffering comes from wrong-doing, as well-being from virtue. If there be suffering in the next world, it is, as in this, but the medicine of the sickly soul."

This is plain. Mr. Parker adopts the opinions of those who are called Universalists on the subject of future retribution. He is wiser than those generally are who think with him. He affirms without argument. Others argue, and in their argument reason sees the fallacy.

We can not but doubt of the sincerity of men who profess to find their religion in the Bible, and yet tell us they believe in no future punishment. The Bible can not be interpreted to favor such views except by subterfuge and perversion on the part of the interpreter. Mr. Parker, therefore, seldom refers to the Bible on this subject. There is at least frankness in the audacity of the skeptic who sets his own reason above the reason of the Bible, and rejects or modifies it when it does not accord with his own conceptions. But to assume that the Bible is in agreement with the doctrine of no future punishment, is a *subtlety* that "perverts the right ways of the Lord," and indicates dishonesty in the interpreter.

We shall give the more attention to this subject, because it is one of vital interest to all persons who enjoy the light of the gospel. It has to do with the motives which deter men from sin. We do not say that Christians act in view of future retribution. Love deters the Christian from sin. For them there is no evil in the future. But for the unthankful and disobedient—for those who abuse the divine mercy and harden themselves in selfishness—there *is* evil in the future; and repentance with such is impossible so long as they believe there is no future punishment. Convince an impenitent man that sin will not exclude him from they mean the same in the other. One thing, therefore, is manifest, *namely*, that the "death" of the wicked will endure as long as the "life" of the righteous. This truth is more obvious than it is in the proposition, six and half a dozen are equal; for in the one case the number is expressed in different language, in the other the same duration is expressed in the same language.

If the Universalist can succeed in proving that the punishment of the wicked will end; he has at the same time proved that the happiness of the righteous will end; because precisely the same words and phrases used to express the one are used to express the other. Thus the dilemma is perfect, and one from which there is no possible escape—that so fast and so far as Mr. Parker is able to destroy, in the minds of the wicked, the fear of *everlasting punishment*, he destroys at the same time, in the minds of all that believe him, the hope of everlasting happiness; because the proof which sustains the one is the same that sustains the other; so that if one fails, both fail—if one stands, both stand—and the duration of the one must remain the same as the duration of the other. Thus, like blind Samson in the temple of the uncircumcised Philistines, if Mr. Parker could succeed in subverting the pillars of the temple of truth, the wreck would fall upon his own head.

There are but two ways by which it is possible to express truth in language. The same truth may be asserted affirmatively and negatively, and when a proposition is proved affirmatively and negatively, it is not possible to make it either stronger or plainer.

Now, the "everlasting punishment" of the impenitent is not only, as proved above, repeatedly affirmed in the word of God; but it is likewise asserted in a negative form, a form by which the existence of God and the happiness of the righteous are also expressed. In relation to God it is written, "Thy dominion shall *not* pass away." In relation to the righteous, they shall receive "a crown of glory that fadeth *not* away." In relation to the wicked, consider the following:

"He that *believeth not* the Son shall *not see life*, but the wrath of God abideth on him."

The blasphemy against the Holy Ghost "*shall not* be forgiven unto men, *neither in this world, neither in the world to come.*"

"In hell he lifted up his eyes, *being in torment.*" "Between us and you there is a great gulf fixed, so that those who would pass from hence to you *can not, neither* can they pass to us who would come from thence."

"Their worm dieth *not*, and their fire is *not quenched*."

"Without holiness *no* man shall see the Lord."

"For if ye believe *not* that I am he ye shall *die in your sins*."

The truth in relation to this topic is, that the same words which are applied in the Bible to teach the eternity of God and the eternity of happiness, are applied to teach the eternity of that "destruction" which shall come upon the wicked. They are the strongest words and phrases which can be used in any language; and all competent interpreters agree that their first import is eternal. And in addition to this, the same truth is taught not only affirmatively but negatively; so that the everlasting punishment of the wicked is proved in the strongest way, and in all the ways that human language can prove any truth.

The Universalists adopt a similar method of interpretation in order to escape the force of the figurative language used in the New Testament. Because the figures which relate to future punishment had a local and temporal origin, they infer that they have only a local and temporal import.

The word translated hell they find originally referred to the valley of the sons of Hinnom, near Jerusalem; hence they confine the figure to its fact, and thus destroy the end for which figures were made. Mr. Parker has not told us whether he adopts the reasoning of those who believe with him in this matter, but as he adopts their conclusions, it is fair to infer he adopts their reasons. Now, if the force of figures is to be destroyed on one side of the argument, it should be on the other; then, supposing this reasoning to be true, there is neither a heaven nor a hell. The word heaven is derived from a word which in its original import signified the atmosphere or the firmament; and the import of the word paradise is a garden. In both cases the words which signify heaven and hell are educed from things temporal and local in their nature. If one must be divested of its meaning, which signifies a state of future punishment, then the other must be divested of its import, which signifies a state of future happiness. We should then, according to this method of interpretation, have neither a hell nor a heaven.

This interpretation strikes at the foundation of revelation. It would be impossible, if such perversions were permitted, for any revelation ever to be made to man. Man can learn the unknown only by figures and parables drawn from the known.

> "For what of God above or man below?
> What can we reason but from what we know?"

No terms are used in the Bible to teach us the existence of a future world, or the condition of the soul in that world, which are not derived in some way from things that pertain to the present state of existence. The Saviour always spake in parables and figures (Matt. xiii. 34), because he had to illustrate the unknown by what was known to his hearers. The individual, therefore, who endeavors to destroy in the minds of his hearers the application of these figures to another life, destroys, so far as he succeeds, the very effect which Christ designed to accomplish by using them. This method of interpretation proves there is no hell, but it proves likewise that there is no devil, no angel, no heaven, no God!

The general tenor of the New Testament—the general acceptation of the words and phrases used by Christ and his apostles, as well as the effects produced by their ministry, render it certain that they taught men that eternal life depended on reconciliation to God as he is manifested in Jesus Christ.

Notice the evidence of this in the following passages.

The points of the following passages are directly against Parkerism. "Fear not them which kill the body, but are not able to kill the soul, but rather fear him which is able to destroy both soul and body in hell."

John v. 25–29. "Marvel not at this, for the hour is coming in the which all that are in their graves shall hear his voice; and shall come forth, they that have done good unto the resurrection of life; and they that have done evil unto the resurrection of damnation.

The judgment is, by the sacred writers, put in order after death, and the resurrection of the dead.

Heb. vi. 2. "The doctrine of baptisms, and of the laying on of hands, and of the resurrection of the dead, and of *eternal judgment.*"

Heb. ix. 27. "And as it is appointed unto men once to die, *but after this the judgment;* so Christ was once offered (or died once), and unto *them which look for him,* shall he appear the *second* time, without sin unto salvation."

2 Tim. iv. 7, 8. "I have fought a good fight, I have finished my course, I have kept the faith; henceforth there is laid up for me a crown of right-

eousness, which the Lord, the righteous judge, will give me at that day; and not to me only, *but unto all them also that love his appearing.*" Was this righteous judgment when Paul would be crowned with "all that loved Christ's appearing," or "all them that looked for him" to be at the destruction of Jerusalem? Or was it then taking place? Either idea is an absurdity.

2 Tim. iv. 1. "I charge thee, therefore, before God and the Lord Jesus Christ, who shall judge the quick [living] and the dead, at his appearing and his kingdom."

2 Pet. ii. 7. "But the heavens and the earth which are now, by the same word are kept in store, reserved unto fire, against the day of judgment and perdition of ungodly men."

By looking at the preceding verses it will be seen that Peter is speaking of the physical earth, affirming its destruction or dissolution once by water, and its final change or dissolution by fire; at which time will be the day of judgment and the "perdition of ungodly men." Observe, he says the present earth is "*kept in store, reserved* unto fire against the day of judgment and perdition of ungodly men." How could language make the truth plainer, that the day of judgment and perdition of ungodly men will be at the time when this earth shall be changed by fire?

2 Peter, ii. 4, 9. "The Lord knoweth how to deliver the godly out of temptation, and to reserve the unjust unto the DAY OF JUDGMENT, to be punished."

Are the unjust rewarded and punished as they go along, and reserved beside unto (not a day, nor this day, nor all days, but) *the day of judgment*, to be punished?

Matth. xii. 32. "Whosoever speaketh a word against the Son of man, it shall be forgiven him. But whosoever speaketh against the Holy Ghost, it shall not be forgiven him, neither in this world nor in the world to come."

John, iii. 16. "For God so loved the world that he gave his only-begotten Son, that whosoever believeth in him should not perish, but have everlasting life." If this does not imply that whosoever does not believe in him *shall perish* and *not have everlasting life*, then there is no meaning in language.

John, vi. 54. "Whosoever eateth my flesh and drinketh my blood hath eternal life, and I will raise him up at the last day." What does this imply, if Christ did not deceive his disciples?

Acts, xxiv. 25. "And as Paul reasoned of righteousness, temperance, and judgment to come, Felix trembled." Was it a judgment that had already come, or the destruction of Jerusalem, that made a *Roman governor* tremble?

1 Peter, iv. 18. "And if the righteous scarcely be saved, where shall the ungodly and the sinner appear?" Easily answered, says Mr. Parker. They will appear in heaven, with the righteous who are scarcely saved.

Matt. xxvi. 24. "It had been good for that man he had not been born." How could this be, if Judas went to heaven at death? If the doctrine that Mr. Parker preaches be true, Judas got to heaven before Jesus.

'He with a cord outwent his Lord,
And got to heaven first."

Luke, x. 42. "But one thing is needful, and Mary hath chosen that good part *that shall never be taken away from her*." Will those who do not choose it have the good part and the one thing needful, which shall never be taken away from them?

James, i. 15. "Then when lust hath conceived, it bringeth forth sin: and sin, when it is finished, bringeth forth *death*." Mr. Parker and the Universalists say that when sin is finished it bringeth forth life. Which is right?

John, viii. 51. "Verily, verily, I say unto you (mark it) if a man keep my sayings he shall never see death." Does this mean the first or the second death—death of the body or of the soul?

It is not doubted by any well-informed person that Christ and his apostles used the words and phrases which those who heard them—those to whom they wrote, would understand as teaching the future punishment of the wicked. They either taught what they believed on this subject, or they willfully deceived the people. They not only used the words which the Jews used to designate future punishment, but they were even careful that the Gentiles should not mistake their meaning. Hence Paul speaks of "blackness of darkness," and Peter uses the word "Tartarus" to convey the same idea.

The whole form and pressure of the apostolic teaching represent themselves and those who heard them as acting under a deep sense of responsibility in regard to the future. "We must all stand before the judgment-seat of Christ." "Knowing the terrors of the Lord, we persuade men." They "warned every man night and day with tears."

Some who heard them "trembled;" others cried out "Men and brethren, what shall we do?" And all believers took up their cross daily and followed Christ—all of them to persecution, and many of them to the flames.

Now, in conclusion of this long letter, I do not know that a vindication of the Scriptures is necessary in your case, and with Mr. Parker it would have little influence. But there are others that it may save from a leap into the darkness of skepticism; and we offer the vindication as a basis of the rational exposition which will ensue.

LETTER IX.

RATIONAL EXPOSITION OF PROBATION AND RETRIBUTION.

MY DEAR SIR:—

The reasonings of those who reject the authority of Scripture while they teach the salvation of all men, are usually predicated upon what *they assume* to be the attributes of God and the parental character of God. Their proposition is as follows: "God is love." He is infinitely wise, infinitely good, and infinitely powerful. He must, therefore, have designed from the beginning the greatest good of all his creatures, and as he has power to execute the designs which his love prompts and his wisdom devises, therefore (they infer) the whole family of man will be saved.

In one sense this proposition is true; but they give it a false sense, and draw from it a false inference. The first fallacy is in the method of their reasoning, which must of necessity produce false results. They start with the *à priori* method, by forming in their own minds a conception of what they choose to imagine the nature and attributes of God ought to be, and then infer results from their own suppositions. Now, every one that knows any thing about the subject knows that the *à posteriori* method, or reasoning from effects to their causes—i. e., induction from the works of God and the Word of God—is the only method by which we can reason with any certainty concerning what the love of God is, or what acts that love would prompt him to accomplish. One man may assume that God is love, and another that he is a God of vengeance; and the reasoning of both concerning what love is, and what vengeance is, will be mere idle or wicked imaginations from beginning to end, unless they define what these words mean when applied to God, by referring to what God does in nature and providence, and what he says in revelation. Nature and revelation both proceed from God, and must, when rightly interpreted, bear true and harmonious testimony to his nature and attributes. The character of the First, or of any cause, not cognizable by the senses, can be known only by the effects which it produces. Vain talkers, by forming in their own minds a character for God, and determining, *à priori*, what kind of religion

God ought to give, and then forcing nature and the Bible to coincide with their speculations, has given rise to more injurious heresies than all other causes combined.

A false method must necessarily lead to a false conclusion. By this method an individual would reason as follows: God is infinitely good and infinitely powerful. As he is infinitely good, he would not desire to create his creatures subject to any evil whatever; and as he is infinitely powerful, he can accomplish all his purposes, therefore all his creatures will be free from all evil, and perfectly happy during their whole existence. But this speculation would lead him into direct falsehood. His reasonings from the supposed character of God would be contradicted both by nature and revelation. And as God is forever the same, the same method of reasoning will forever lead to falsehood as its result.

Let us, by a better logic, endeavor to reach a result more in accordance with experience and the Bible. The Scriptures affirm that "God is love," and as the results which skeptics deduce from their own assumptions on this subject are contradicted both by natural and revealed truth, the vital questions arise, What is the love of God? and, In what manner is the love of God manifested? The Scriptures teach "God is love," "Our God is a consuming fire," "His name is holy." The living creatures before the throne, full of eyes within, denoting profound and pervading intelligence, cry continually, "Holy, holy, holy, is the Lord God Almighty." Holiness is applied to God more emphatically, more frequently, and in a greater variety of language, than any other word in the Scriptures. The love of God, then, is holy love, or love of holiness. Now, if holy love is the character of God, then his character is directly opposed to sin. It is a truism that God must be opposed by nature to whatever is opposed to his nature. It belongs to the nature of things, that just in proportion as any being loves one thing, he is opposed to that which is its opposite. Hence it follows that God can not love holiness without hating sin, just in proportion to his love of holiness. The principle is so obvious that every sane mind will assent to it. This truth is not only matter of principle, but it is matter of fact. We know the more holy—the more like God a Christian becomes, the more he hates sin. It is likewise matter of necessity, because sin is the opposite of holiness, and love is the opposite of hatred. It is likewise matter of revelation; Jesus said, "If a man love the one he will hate the other, ye can not serve God and mammon." From these premises then, it follows, that the more any being loves holiness, the more he hates sin ; and the conclusion follows incontrovertibly and eternally, that as God has infinite love for holiness, he is infinitely opposed to sin.

If, then, God's nature is holy love, how would the love of God be manifested toward the human family, who are sinners? The answer is plain in two respects—(1) It would be manifested in a manner consistent with the nature and wants of man; and (2) it would be manifested in a manner adapted to turn man from sin to holiness. Man can find happiness only in holiness. God is love, and would seek man's happiness only by making him holy. There is a physical necessity in the one case, and a moral necessity in the other. There is, first, the necessity of nature. The beaver is so constituted, that he finds his happiness in the water; and if he were by some means thrown upon the land, no benefit could be conferred upon him that would make him happy, and answer the ends of his nature, only that he should be led back to the water. His constitution was such, that no other benefit would do him permanent good. If a physician were called to see a patient who had a cancer on his breast, the only thing to be done would be to cut it out from the roots. The physician might give palliatives, so that the patient would have less pain —or he might make his patient believe it was no cancer—or forget that he had a cancer near his vitals; but if the physician were to do this instead of removing the evil, he would be a wicked man and the enemy of his patient. The man's case was such, that the only favor which could be conferred upon him would be to cut out the cancer. Now all agree that sin is the great evil of the soul of man. Nothing can make man spiritually happy here, or fit him for happiness hereafter, but the removal of sin from his nature. Sin is the plague-spot on the soul which destroys its peace, and threatens its destruction unless removed. It is therefore certain that if the love of God were manifested toward man, it would be in turning man from sin, which produces misery, to holiness which produces happiness.

The question that remains is, in what way, consistently with the nature of man, would the love of God be manifested in using means and influences to turn men from sin to holiness?

All revelation, as well as philosophy and experience, teach that man is a sinner;—but God holy. Now, if God is holy and man is a sinner, two things follow of course. First that the will of man differs from the will of God; second, that God desires the will of man should be conformed to his will. The question then arises, by what method would God's goodness be manifested in influencing the will of man to accord with his own will as revealed to us in reason and the Bible? The answer to this question is obvious, both from reason and revelation.

The will of man can be influenced but in two ways, viz., by compulsion and by motives. A man might be forced to sign a deed, or say his prayers, or to obey by external action some commandment; yet his acts would have no moral character. The only way that a man's will can be moved, and he continue a moral agent, is by motives. The will of man *never acts morally* except in view of motives. It follows, then, that as it is God's desire that man, as a free agent, should love and obey him—the evidence of his goodness is just in proportion to the motives which he has presented to turn him from evil to good. For it being true that the will of man in his present condition may be influenced to good or evil by motives—and it being likewise true that sin is an evil which destroys the happiness or life of the soul—then it is obvious that that being manifests the most goodness, who presents the strongest motives to man, *as a free agent*—to deter him from sin and influence him to holiness; and that is a wicked being, and the enemy of God and man, who destroys the motives which would influence men from sin to holiness.

Further, the soul is so constituted that it can be influenced by motives in two ways, viz., by addressing its hopes and its fears. Now, if God has so constituted the soul, that it can be influenced by motives from evil to good in these two ways, it is conclusive evidence of his goodness that he has in both these ways used means to influence the minds of his creatures. And the stronger the motives thus presented, the stronger the evidence of the goodness of God. Now, from these premises, mark the motives which God has set before sinners in the Bible. To *deter them from sin*, God has presented for their consideration the everlasting punishment of devils and disobedient sinners; and to influence them to good, he has set before them the everlasting blessedness of those who repent, and love and obey him. Both of these being motives alike designed to influence men from sin to holiness, the man who denies the existence of a hell, denies the evidence of the goodness of God as truly as the man who denies the existence of heaven.

Everlasting punishment and the perdition of ungodly men, as the consequence of sin, and involving suffering in proportion to their sins, is the greatest motive that can be addressed to men to deter them from evil; and everlasting life and happiness the greatest that can be presented to induce them to good.

In presenting these motives, God has given the highest evidence of his goodness and love to his creatures; because he has presented infinite motives to induce them to heaven and happiness; and presented them in every way by which they can affect the will. On the one side there is the everlasting punishment of hell, as the consequence of *sin*, and on the other the blessedness of heaven, as the consequence of holiness, through the mercy of Christ; and he that will continue to disobey God, notwithstanding these motives, deserves to go to hell, and must go there from the necessity of the case, because no greater motives than everlasting punishment and everlasting happiness can be presented to influence the will of an intelligent free agent; and no greater kindness can be manifested to move the heart than the voluntary sacrifice of Jesus for man. If the sinner will not repent and love God, in view of these, nothing but physical force remains, and God will never force sinners by physical means to heaven and happiness.

We do not design to say that the fear of punishment is a motive which induces Christians to obey. "The love of God casteth out fear." There is no punishment for the children of God, therefore they have nothing to fear. It is for those who disobey and pervert God's truth to fear hell. God has told them the consequence of their sin in order that they may be arrested in their course of transgression. Before them in the way to hell stands the angel of justice, holding up the holy law, in which it is written, "Repent or perish." Behind them, in the way to heaven, stands the divine Saviour, crying, "*Turn ye, turn ye*—for why will ye die?" A sense of evil and danger arrests the sinner—love reforms and guides the saint.

Man is a being of hopes and fears, and God has addressed him as such in the Bible; and it can not be doubted that if there were no motives in the gospel addressed to the fears of men to turn them from evil, that God might have influenced men in one way which has not been done. Consequently, by denying the existence of everlasting punishment, Mr. Parker denies that God has presented infinite motives to deter men from sin; instead, therefore, of showing the infinite goodness of God, he makes a direct attack upon the goodness of Jehovah ; and an attack which, so far as successful, destroys the power of the gospel, by destroying the motives by which God would influence men to repentance. And this is done notwithstanding that terrible anathema which God has thundered in the ears of all those who pervert his truth—"If any man preach any other gospel unto you than that ye have received—*let him be accursed.*"

The existence of future punishment and "everlasting destruction," is an evidence of the goodness, justice, and wisdom of God : of goodness, in that it is a motive to prevent sin and turn men from evil; of justice, in that it is the righteous doom of irreclaimable sinners; and of wisdom, in that God can thus make the penalty of sin a motive to deter from sin.

And the fact that all these divine means, and motives, and influences are used in this world to turn men from sin to holiness, teaches us that this world is a place of probation—the place where God's long-suffering spares men in order that they may repent and obey the gospel. If in view of forbearance and infinite mercy and motives on the part of God, they will not be saved, the only alternative is that they be permitted to sin and suffer the consequence. In the intermediate state they will suffer in proportion to the sinfulness of their character, and when "death and hell deliver up their dead every one not found written in the Lamb's Book of Life will be cast into the lake of fire, which is the second death."

The existence of hell may even be, in one sense, an evidence of God's mercy as well as his justice. It may be the best thing that can be done for natures which have confirmed themselves in sin. Suppose it had been proposed to Benedict Arnold, after his apostasy, to return to the colonies—ask the pardon of Washington—confess his wicked duplicity and treachery, and on these conditions be restored to citizenship. He would have known that such a course would promote his happiness, yet without a change of principle, he would have rejected it with contempt. Suppose further, that when the war was finished, and Washington had put down all power adverse to the happiness of the colonies, Arnold was found among the prisoners, having contended as long as he could against the government. His situation was now such, that any confession that he might make, or any pardon for which he might ask, could proceed from no other than selfish motives. When men fall into the hands of the living God, or into the hands of the executor of the law, repentance and love to the lawgiver is then impossible, because the motive determines the character of the act, and right motives in acting would then be impossible, because they would be necessarily selfish.

Now, then, seeing repentance and love for the governor under such circumstances would be impossible, suppose the alternative had been proposed to Arnold either to spend his life in the presence of Washington, and in the society of those who knew him to be a traitor at heart; or to be banished to an island which contained only rebels and criminals like himself, he would undoubtedly have chosen the latter immediately. Because, although the island would be a hell on account of the remorse of guilty consciences and the rage of evil passions that would exist and increase there, yet his nature had become so corrupted, that to live under the eye of the magnanimous Washington, and amid those who abhorred bad principles, would have been to his soul severer punishment than to live among the guilty and condemned in the island.

Now, suppose Washington (knowing that his apostasy had so corrupted his nature that he would be less miserable to be banished from his presence than to continue in the society that made patriots happy), in view of his past life, and in view of the character he then possessed, had banished him forever from his presence, such banishment would have been not only an exhibition of justice but of mercy, and it would have been the best thing that could have been done for the man in view of his character and circumstances. So with God. Banishment to hell is the best thing that can be done for those who die in rebellion; therefore God has, in justice and mercy, provided a hell for fallen angels and impenitent sinners, who die unpardoned and unreconciled to God, as revealed in Christ Jesus.

These views, then, present the love of God in the only rational light—consistent with justice and with the principles of righteous moral government—with the nature of man, and especially with the revelation of God. In the light of the subject as thus exhibited, the revelation of truth, the existence of conscience, the influence of the church of Christ, the motives of the gospel, the power of the atonement, and the influence of the Holy Ghost, are all direct evidences of the love of God. And the wickedness of individuals, notwithstanding these manifestations of mercy, in refusing to repent and put their confidence in Christ, renders it necessary that they should be damned, because they will not be saved in consistency with their own nature, nor with justice, nor with the moral government of God.

Another form of argument, constantly reiterated, is stated as follows:

God is the Father of all men. A good father, if he had the power, would not permit his children to suffer except for their own good. God has the power, and therefore will permit no suffering except for the good or the reformation of his offspring.

In the assemblies of Universalists and Rationalists this appeal is constantly made to the partialities, prejudices, and sympathies of parents; and by this method as much as any other, they pervert the truth and beguile unstable minds into error.

This position is untrue in both its parts. God does not act toward the family of man as a good earthly parent would act toward his children if he had the power; nor can he do so, as we shall see, without a direct violation of the principles of truth and righteousness. A good earthly parent, if he had the power, would not allow his child to become a thief, or a debauchee, or a blasphemer, or a murderer; yet God, having the power to prevent it, does permit men to commit every degree of crime. A good earthly parent would not permit his children to suffer excruciating pain by fire, accident, or poison, yet God permits these. A good earthly parent, if he had the power to prevent it, would not allow one child to oppress another, nor would he allow his children to become insane, or to blaspheme the name of their father, or to injure his interests; yet God has the power, and allows all these things among the human family. And if the condition of all be alike hereafter, God is unjust to permit one child to make another miserable during their whole life in this world, and then receive both to equal blessedness hereafter.

But further, it would be unjust in God if he were to treat all men as earthly parents, under the influence of their parental instincts, treat their children.

God has for wise purposes implanted in the hearts of parents peculiar instincts. These instincts are constitutional, as they are in animals, and they lead parents to feel peculiar attachments and partialities for their own children, which they do not feel for the children of others. This natural instinct has been recognized as partial in all ages. It is recognized in all courts of justice as disqualifying parents and children for testifying for or against each other. While parents would insist upon the execution of the law upon others, their parental instincts would lead them to resist its execution upon their own children. Those who hear the appeal of false teachers upon this subject never stop to reflect that it charges God with injustice. Earthly parents are partial—God is impartial. Suppose, for instance, that in some neighborhood a young man should rebel against the laws, and commit murder, or some crime worthy of imprisonment for life. His own father would shelter him from the just penalty of the law, and use every means that his son might go "unwhipped of justice." But what would the other fathers in the neighborhood do? These would use all diligence to bring the guilty individual to the justice which his crimes merited. They would even enter his father's house and commit him to the officers of the law. Now, in this case, which did right? Every honest man says, those who brought the culprit to justice; while the father who concealed his son, acting as a parent, was "partial" and a "respecter of persons." Now, shall man be more just than God? And yet skeptics delude their hearers by comparing the justice of Jehovah, who is "no respecter of persons," to the natural sympathies of this earthly parent. Will it not be great mercy in God to forgive such outrages upon his character; especially after he has plainly said, Rom. ii. 6, that he "will render to every man according to his deeds—to them who by *patient continuance* in well doing seek for glory, and honor, and immortality, *eternal life;* but unto them that are contentious, and obey not the truth, but obey unrighteousness, indignation and wrath, tribulation and anguish, upon *every soul* of man that doeth evil; of the Jews first, and also of the Gentiles."

Nor are men the children of God in the sense that Adam was the son of God. God was the immediate creator both of the soul and body of Adam. The first man was created holy, possessing the moral image of his Maker, and was the son of God in a sense in which Adam's posterity are not.

Nor is it true that all men are the children of God in the same sense that Christians who are born of the Spirit are the sons of God. Like many of our day, the Jews, who denied the divinity of Christ, and expected salvation without repentance and faith, claimed that they were the children of God, and that God was their father. They said to Jesus (John, viii. 41–47), "We be not born of fornication, *we have one father, even God.*" The reply of Christ to this assumption of wicked men ought to put to shame Universalists, Rationalists, and all others, who, without faith and the love of God, which produce obedience, yet claim to be God's children. Said Jesus to such individuals, "Ye are of your father the devil, and the lusts of your father ye will do," etc.

THE TRUE VIEWS.

God is the Universal Creator. "All things were made by Christ, and without him was not any thing made that was made." Man was distinguished from the creatures by being created in the moral image of God, "in righteousness and true holiness." After God had created the original parents of the races, he instituted those laws, in accordance with which they perpetuated their earthly existence. By his sin man lost his holiness and his *birthright*, and the moral image of God, in which he was created, was effaced from his soul. The steps by which he fell (mark them) were—*First.* Under evil influence he was led to doubt the truth of God's word. *Second.* Under the influence of this doubt he turned from holiness to disobedience. Now, in order to his restoration, he must return by precisely the same steps by which he departed; only the agency under which he acts is the opposite one, and the steps the opposite way. *First.* Under the influence of the Holy Spirit he must place his confidence again in God's Word, i. e., have faith in Christ; and, *second*, under the influence of this faith, he must return to obedience, i. e., must repent. Man must be born again of the Spirit, and then he will have Christ, the image of God, again "formed in his soul, the hope of glory." (John, i. 12, 13.) "As many as received him, to them gave he power to become the sons of God, even to them that believe on his name; which were born, not of blood," i. e., not by natural generation; "nor of the will of the flesh," i. e., not by the power or self-determination of the fleshly or carnal will; "nor of the will of man," i. e., not by the power of moral suasion, nor by the efforts of the will of men over each other; "but of God," i. e., renewed by the Holy Ghost. The sons of God are those who are born again of the Spirit through the truth. None are the children of God, and God is a Father to none in the spiritual sense, except those who are willing to separate themselves from the unbelieving and disobedient, and by faith and repentance become as little children. (See 2 Cor. vi. 14, 18.)

When individuals are thus restored to the favor of God, and the image of God is restored to their souls, then they become "heirs of God, and joint-heirs with Jesus Christ." They have the privileges, the blessings, and the inheritance of children, and God covenants as their father to overrule all things for the good of his obedient children (Rom. viii. 28), and when it is necessary, in order to their spiritual good, he chastens them as a good father does his children, and in a manner in which those are not disciplined who are called in the Scriptures the "children of this world—the children of disobedience—the children of the devil." (See 1 Cor. xi. 32; Heb. xii. 6–8.)

LETTER X.

REFUTATION OF COMMON FALLACIES ON THE SUBJECT OF FUTURE RETRIBUTION.

MY DEAR SIR:—

We are told, as noticed in a preceding letter, that "the woes of sin are but its antidote. Suffering comes from wrong-doing, as well-being from virtue. If there be suffering in the next world, it is, as in this, but the medicine for the sickly soul," p. 438.

In the above sentence the usual method of the author is adopted. Truth is adroitly mingled with error. The fallacy of disciplinary punishment, as a cure for sin, and the hope of universal salvation, is propagated in a form of words which, in proper connections, would teach a general truth. All good men believe that "suffering comes from wrong-doing, as well-being from virtue;" but it does not therefore follow that the woes of sin are its antidote, either in this world or the next.

It is true, no doubt, that good men are punished

for their sins in this world; their discipline produces reform, and fits them for heaven. But it does not follow that the woes of sin produce the same effect upon the impenitent mind. Such a result in the case of those who are not converted is impossible, *because it is by faith that discipline from the divine Father becomes a good in the soul.* In the case of those who have faith, a Father's hand and a Father's love are seen in adverse providences. They receive them as discipline, and are brought by them into a penitent and filial temper; and thus temporal afflictions are, as a matter of experience, a means of separating a believing mind from evil. But in the case of those who are "without faith and without God in the world," temporal afflictions do not produce piety. *God does not design to reform sinners by the woes of sin. If he does, he fails in his object; because some men sin, and suffer the woes of sin all their lives, and grow worse and worse till they die.* If, therefore, God disciplined them in order to reform them, the effort was worse than a failure, because instead of making them better, it made them worse.

It is not only a fact which all but the morally blind can see, that the discipline which is a "savor of life unto life" with some, is a "savor of death unto death" with others; but it is likewise a distinctly revealed doctrine of the New Testament. "God knows how to deliver the godly out of temptation, and to reserve the unjust unto the day of judgment to be punished." The inspired writer says to his fellow-Christians, "When *we* are afflicted we are chastened of the Lord, that we may not be *condemned with the world.*" So far, then, as this world is concerned, it is matter of experience and of revelation that while the woes of sin are a moral discipline and a moral benefit to one class, they do not benefit the other.

That wicked and worldly men often repent when they feel the consequences of their wrong-doing, there is no doubt. But selfish repentance "worketh death." Instead of making men better, it makes them worse. They sorrow because they have injured *themselves.* Such repentance is selfish, and fits men for hell. "The sorrow of the world worketh death." The effects of sinning upon selfish minds make them worse instead of better; and so far as Mr. Parker leads unregenerated men to believe that the woes they experience in consequence of their sins will be a cure of sin, he aids to fit them for the "second death." These are solemn words, but they are true.

Now, without dwelling further on the philosophical blunder, which any thoughtful mind should be ashamed to commit, i. e., that an effect will change or *cure* its cause, let me invite your attention to another aspect in which this doctrine of Mr. Parker (a doctrine held likewise by Emerson, Chapin, and all the Transcendentalists and Universalists in general) is opposed both to experience and revelation.

It may be said—(because in view of preceding facts it must be admitted that temporal providences do not reform sinners)—it may be said that the *moral* relations of things, or the "*operations of man's moral nature,*" will cure sin in his soul. Now, we shall show that this fallacy is as absurd as the preceding.

Instead of sin being a self-destructive, it is a self-strengthening and self-perpetuating principle. Instead of the consequences of a sinful act tending to cure the sinful propension, it actually strengthens it. After one sin, another is more easily and more readily committed; because the sinful act weakens the conscience, confirms a sinful habit, and strengthens the propension to sin in the soul. As a matter of fact, sin blinds the moral vision, and kills the moral sense. The more sinful any individual becomes, the less he *sees* and the less he *feels* of the evil of sin. This momentous moral fact can not be denied. It is a natural law—the law of divine judgment—and so long as it is true, the statement that the effect of sinning cures sin is a falsehood uttered in the face of law, experience, and the Scriptures.

The doctrine that conscience punishes men for sin is an impeachment of the justice of God. If this were true, in order that God might be just, the greatest sinner should be the greatest sufferer. But the opposite of this is true. A good man will suffer more for neglecting his prayers, than a bad one will feel for the crime of profaneness. If conscience is the measure of God's justice, then the divine being loves the wicked more than he loves the good; because the more holy the mind, the more potent is conscience—the less holy, the less the infliction. If "men are punished as they go along," and suffer in this world in proportion to their sin, then, as we have said before, Jesus Christ was the greatest of sinners, because he was the greatest of sufferers.

The fact that conscience dies as sin increases, but grows strong in proportion to holiness, shows, by human experience, what is affirmed in the Scriptures, that the good are punished in this world, while the evil are reserved unto the day of judgment to be punished.

"But," says our philosopher, "suffering comes from wrong-doing, as well-being from virtue." Now, if this fact renders it doubtful whether there be any future punishment, it renders it doubtful, in the same measure, whether there be any future happiness. If sin punishes itself, virtue rewards itself. And if sin ceases to punish itself at death, then virtue ceases to reward itself at death; so that there is neither rewards nor punishments—neither a hell nor a heaven, in the life to come.

If the woes of sin will make men good, then the joys of goodness will make them bad. So in the next world. We are told that if there be any suffering, it is but the medicine of the sick soul, i. e., it cures sin; then the same reasoning is valid in regard to heaven. If there be any enjoyment there, it makes the soul sick by sin: thus hell fits the soul for heaven, and heaven fits the soul for hell, one as much as the other. And we defy any man to show that the foundation for the argument is not as good on one side as it is on the other. If the soul, by the practice of sin will make itself holy, then certainly the soul, by the practice of virtue, will make itself sinful.

Let us look, in conclusion, at the facts which are connected with the subject of sin and retribution. What are the effects of sin in this life? and—Do the effects of sin continue in the future world?

The answers to these inquiries are plain both from reason and the Scriptures. Sin produces two results in the soul. It produces present evil, while at the same time it fits the character for future retribution. Just as benevolent action produces peace and complacency of soul in the present life, and forms the soul into a benevolent character, which fits it for heaven. Every one knows—Mr. Parker knows—that while sin produces more or less unrest when the act is done; it likewise, by the same act, fixes character. Like a stream which, running constantly over a rock, wears for itself a channel from which in the end it can not escape, so the soul, by continued action of a selfish or sensual nature, forms a habit which fixes its mode of action for the future. Now, destiny depends upon character. A benevolent heart is happy in its own exercises; a selfish mind is confirming a character which destroys happiness, or rather which renders happiness impossible. All men act either from a selfish motive or a benevolent one. Every selfish act confirms a selfish character, and the man who dies having confirmed a selfish character by a selfish life, is fitted for hell; and as death is not a change of the soul but a change of the body, he will experience hell forever, unless God annihilate him after the judgment.

Is it said now, as a final lie, that so soon as the soul is separated from sense, and experiences in the next world the evil consequences of sin, these evil consequences will lead to repentance. We answer that repentance in view of the experience of evil or the fear of evil, is repentance toward self, not toward God. The more men repent from an experience of evil consequences, the more they are damned. The thief always repents when the sheriff arrests him. Death forces many men to submit, others to repent. Such repentance is by necessity, or in view of consequences, not in view of God's goodness and of the *evil* of sin. Some weak people talk of repentance on the gallows. Dying sinners and murderers often repent, but it is a repentance forced in view of the termination of their moral agency. In this world "repentance toward God" works by reformation; and faith in our Lord Jesus Christ works by love. In the world of doom, when moral probation is ended, repentance, by the necessity of the case, works by remorse; and faith by trembling. "The devils believe in one God and tremble."

Character is the only hope of heaven. Character that begins with "repentance unto life," and is formed by benevolent aspiration and action—character which is conformed to the divine law, and governed by benevolent motive—which motive is begotten only by faith in God, as manifested in Christ Jesus.

The last thought in the foregoing paragraph brings us to a vital point in the divine process of human salvation. It introduces Christ as the motive power, without which the soul is destitute of divine life. It will admit of a homily, which you will suffer me to give in conclusion.

One of the darkest developments of Mr. Parker's infidelity—a development which indicates cardinal alienation from Christian character in all those who sympathize with it—is the contempt and hostility manifested toward the self-sacrifice of Christ as the motive and the merit by which men are saved. In words which caricature the Christian creed, while they convey the hostility of the author to the Christian faith, it is written in the introduction of "Discourses of Religion," p. 5 (speaking of the evils of the prevailing religious ideas): "We dare not approach the Infinite one face to face. We whine and whimper in our brother's name, as though we could only approach the Infinite One by attorney." And again, page 432, "Can men approach the Everywhere-present only by attorney, as a beggar comes to a Turkish king? Away with such folly. Christ bears his own sins, not another's."

Has Mr. Parker forgotten that it is one of the most explicit commands of Christ, that after his sacrifice and ascension, his disciples should always make their supplications in his name. John, xvi. 22–27—"And in that day ye shall ask me nothing. Verily, verily, I say unto you, whatsoever ye shall ask the Father in my name, he will give it you [ch. xiv. 13, "I will do it"]. Hitherto ye have asked nothing in my name. Ask, and ye shall receive, that your joy may be full." "At that day ye shall ask in my name, and I say not unto you that I will pray the Father for you, for the Father himself loveth you, because ye have loved me, and have believed that I came out from God."

In accordance with this command is the practice of the apostles and of the church of Christ in all ages.

The scoffing of Thomas Paine was more fair in language and less repulsive in spirit than that of Mr. Parker. Thomas Paine believed in future retribution, and, in stating the views of Christians, he did not usually pervert them. We should be glad if as much could be said of Mr. Parker and other Universalists and Transcendentalists. It is easy to caricature the most sacred doctrines. The doctrine that Christ is Mediator between God and men is philosophical, experimental, and scriptural. Mr. Parker does not argue in opposition to this. The logical faculty is not developed in the Carlyle school to which he belongs. He "utters" his "intuitions" in words which men whose feelings are hostile to the gospel will love, because they travestie the truth.

We say the doctrine of Christ's mediation is a truth which commends itself to the reason, as it does to the moral wants of men. [See Phil. of Plan of Salvation, and Book II. of "God in Christ."] All spirit, so far as we know, affects other spirits through organization. How does Mr. Parker know but that Christ is the medium (if we may so speak) by which God comes in contact with matter? We know that he is the medium by which God unites himself with humanity. "There is one God and one Mediator between God and men—the man Christ Jesus." The human soul operates through corporeal media upon other minds; and upon matter it operates through more remote instrumentalities. Media of communication between the inferior and superior is the order of nature. Is not the divine Mediator in this order? or does God contravene the order he has himself established?

It is a law of creation that substances as well as spirits come together by affinity. If matter or spirit of different affinities ever be united, a new medium, or solvent, must be found by which the diverse qualities may be reconciled or harmonized. But Mr. Parker wants no mediator between him and the Most Holy—no reconciliation of the earth-born to the Eternal—no solvent of the imperfect earthly that it may melt into the bosom of Infinite Love.

Blessed be God, there is a more rational and a holier faith than this. The revealed Christ is the Mediator in the order of nature, and in the ordination of grace. God, by the mediation of Christ, unites himself with our earthly and imperfect nature, and by faith the soul is transformed from a lower to a celestial species. On one side—the divinity—God comes in. On the other, the humanity, man comes in; so that God and man are reconciled in Christ. "God was in Christ reconciling the world unto himself."

Mr. Parker ridicules the idea of approaching God in the name of Jesus, and tells us that "he died for his own sins!" (Such phraseology is wicked, but it needs a reply as well as a rebuke.) We are so constituted, that benevolent action is impossible with the human mind unless the motive-power which moves the will be drawn from another, not from ourselves. The man who lives and acts in view of Christ is God-moved; that is, his soul is exercised by the character of God manifested in Christ Jesus. The man who has no faith is self-moved. His own will is supreme, and not God's will. Hence he is a rebel in the moral government of God. When we love another, we are willing to deny ourselves in order to conform to the object of our regard. This takes the motive out of ourselves. If the will of that other is incarnate love, the soul moved by it becomes benevolent, *and the soul can become benevolent in no other way.* Until this is accomplished, every act of life is selfish; and thus life-action is death-action, which fits the soul for the second death.

For Christ's sake, then, is only another expression for the great truth, that all our holy motions and emotions are dependent on him. "In Christ's name" is a recognition that God is manifest in his sacrifice for sin, and that it is in his mercy alone that we have hope. In all systems there are two motions of subordinate bodies, one on their own axis, the other around the central orbit; so in the spiritual world, the soul is self-moved, and the regenerated soul moves likewise in its orbit of dependence on God. To feel reliance on the merit of Christ—*to trust in his name*—is the expression of this actual and practical relation. The man who does not feel it is dead.

Thus the mind that draws its motive from Christ is a restored spirit. The affinity between the divine and human mind is re-united, and the soul takes on its eternal movement around the infinite center of life and love.

O holy One, who hath manifested thy mercy to us in Christ Jesus, in thy name and in thy merit we trust for motive to move our will, mercy to affect our heart, and for grace to pardon our sin; and not unto us, but unto thee, be the glory.

Yours in the heart of the *gospel.*

LETTER XI.

REFORMERS AND THEIR RELATION TO CHRISTIANITY.

MY DEAR SIR:—

In the first letter of this correspondence I had occasion to advert to Mr. Parker as a reformer, and in that connection to speak with proper respect of his principles and the value of his labors. I mentioned that in the introduction of his name in many cases, I used it as the representative of a class. I wish you so to understand it still. While it is true that his published opinions represent, to some extent, all the heresies and moral vagaries of the times, yet as he is not "alone in his glory" in relation to many things of which we have spoken, and are now about to speak, we design that you should apply our remarks to others, and to yourself, so far as you "muster in the same company."

I wish in this letter to present in a connected and more extended form what I believe to be the true value of reform effort, and the relation of benevolent reforms to the gospel of Christ. I am sorry to know that your present alienation from many with whom you once labored is occasioned, in part at least, by what you believe to be "a defection from the principles of justice and mercy on the part of those who claim to be, *par excellence*, the disciples of Christ." Now, I admit your charge, and approve the sentiment, if not the spirit, of your censure in some cases; but the facts that seem to have alienated you from gospel fellowship, bind me more devoutly to gospel truth and influence as our only hope.

While I indorse, to some extent, the denouncements which you and Mr. Parker utter against those who, professing to be Christians, yet by their silence, or in other ways, "give aid and comfort to evil-doers;" still, there is often a spirit of indiscriminate denouncement and of uncharitableness of speech which indicates something else than the "mind of Christ" in the reprover.

Let the defection of professing Christians on the subject of reforms be distinctly condemned. There are cases which can not be contemplated by right-minded men without pity and abhorrence. The studied silence of ministers and whole denominations in regard to one of the most demoralizing and anti-republican institutions under the sun—the gross inconsistencies of great church courts which condemn and disfellowship dancers and such like offenders while they fellowship actual sinners—the defection of some who were true to humanity in the beginning, but have been perverted by public sentiment, or awed into silence by worldly influences—the purchase of others by great boards or church powers, by offering them secretaryships, editorships, and such like bribes—such cases are repulsive not only to Christians but to all upright minds. I do not believe as you do, that "Jesus would class such men with Judas, as 'a devil' whom the popular church power bought to betray his master;" yet that Jesus would look with disapprobation, if not with anger, on such men, I can not doubt.

How far there may be palliation or apology for such cases of defection, it is difficult to see. To apologize for wrong-doing weakens the moral sentiment against wrong. The wisest way for individual Christians and churches to do, would be to follow the advice of Albert Barnes (which he has not followed himself), and separate themselves from all church bodies and boards which tolerate and sanctify sin by giving it the communion.

Great church organizations are thought to be expedient, but they must, from the nature of the case, embody in their extended limits much of worldly influence and of sin. Many of them have power to give men place and position. Hence they become the objects of idolatrous regard with some, and their sentiment and power control many others. It is not strange, therefore, that men of aspiring minds, who are dependent on them in a measure for position or reputation, should endeavor to propitiate their power, even so far as to tolerate and apologize for the sins which great bodies include in their bosom. "They sacrifice to their net, and burn incense unto their drag, because by them their portion is fat, and their meat plenteous." Hab. i. 16.

But the true Christian, while he sees the cause and deplores the consequence in such individual cases, does not, therefore, denounce all church organization and all evangelical Christianity. Many who followed Christ when he announced to them popular truth, went back and walked no more with him when he announced unpopular truth. And one of the most enlightened of his professed friends betrayed him on the charge of being the enemy of the government. But would it have been wise in the men of that age, while they condemned this defection and wickedness, to have refused allegiance to Jesus as "the only name given under heaven among men, by which they must be saved?" On one such occasion Jesus said to the few faithful ones, "Will ye also go away?" One answered, "Lord, to whom shall we go? thou hast the words of eternal life?" The apostacy of those men, whose motive is corrupted by worldly sentiment, or church power, will only lead the true heart to cling more closely to its master.

Let us, therefore, endeavor to discriminate in individual cases, between what is good and evil in this matter. I shall follow your objections and allegations for the most part, but shall not deem it necessary to quote, in an extended form, your words. I wish to give your allegations all the force they deserve, while I show at the same time that in the evangelical doctrine and power of our holy religion is the only hope of good to men.

You speak of Christian ministers as "more Judaic than Christian, more orthodox than evangelical in their sentiments." This I have no doubt is true of some of the prominent theologians of this and other countries. By a strange hallucination, the introductory and imperfect system of Moses is made, in many instances, the higher law in seeking an exposition of the teachings of Jesus. The spirit of both the Old and the New Testaments condemns such a method of exposition. The Old Testament, in its later periods especially, looked joyfully to clearer light in the future. The New declared that "the law made nothing perfect," else it would not have been superseded. *Grace and truth are by Jesus Christ.* The error of interpreting the divine teachings of Jesus in accordance with a darker dispensation, and especially in accordance *with the deteriorated principles and life of the church in this age*, is one of the evils of our times. It is an error that has prevailed in all ages, just in proportion as the church has become worldly and wicked. The most hopeful aspect of the age is, that a protest against this and kindred abuses of the gospel is rising to heaven, while it is stirring the hearts of thousands upon earth. It gathers strength and volume, and betokens a period of coming renovation.

But it is likewise said that we are more orthodox than evangelical. The charge is true only in some cases. Orthodoxy without evangelism has been the bane of the church in all ages. The Scribes and Pharisees sat in Moses' seat, and in forms of faith and non-essentials, their teaching was correct; and yet Jesus denounced them as the enemies of love and righteousness. The orthodox *un*evangelical divines are the most subtle and difficult enemies that the true church of Christ has to deal with. In the days of Edwards they resisted and persecuted him. So they did Wesley; so they did Whitefield. Now they build their tombs and laud their piety, and at the same time persecute and denounce other men of like spirit. In the next age the orthodox but *un*-evangelical theologians will build the tomb of Edwards and Finney, and persecute some other man of God that denounces the sins of his age, whether in the church or out of it.

What we want is not less orthodoxy, but more of Christ's spirit—more love, more power in the hearts of the ministry. The devil may be orthodox, but not evangelical. The form of godliness without its power, is the curse of the church and the world. There are many churches, especially in our cities, from which the poor are excluded as really as though one of the elders stood at the door with a club, to strike every man who did not have the mark of the world on his forehead. Such arrangements are from beneath, not from above; and many of those who worship there, if they have any object, have only a selfish one—to add heaven to their other possessions, just as they would add another farm to their domain. If Christ's gospel is true, self-seeking, lower law, orthodox, *un*evangelical teachers, and such selfish worshipers, are not ministers, or members, such as are required in the New Testament church. Do not understand me as denouncing the ministry and the churches. God forbid! Jesus did not mean to denounce the true church when he reprobated the formal, selfish, hypocritical majority of the Jewish teachers and worshipers. There are hundreds of true ministers and thousands of true Christians in the churches; and true Christians are nowhere else; but now, as in Christ's time, they have to fight with powers and principalities,—with "spiritual wickedness" in the church; as well as "the world, the flesh, and the devil" out of the church.

In my opinion, a reformer who is endeavoring to promote liberty and love in the world, is much better than a professor who turns a cold shoulder to benevolent reforms. The one, without a profession of the gospel, does by nature some things written in the gospel. The other professing the gospel, denies its spirit.

It may be asked, then, "What advantage hath the Christian?" "Much, every way." His advantages are eminent and vital. Let us see.

Society can receive its final moral renovation *only by Christianity*, and reforms can triumph in the end only through Christian faith. Seneca and Plato, who represent the highest moral attainment without Christianity, say nothing about the wickedness of slaveholding, and nothing about the intrinsic selfishness of living for the good of the individual or class, and not for the good of the family of man. They do not announce the principles of fraternity and equality, nor do they *reveal a faith which works by love to God and men.* They do not require those who have means, light, liberty, to make self-denials to confer the advantages they possess on those deprived of them. They did not send forth epistles to urge the world to worship a common Father, and to require men to labor for each other, as a common brotherhood. They did not say, "Love your enemies," "Resist not evil," "God is love, and he that loveth is born of God." Yet *these are the vital elements of all true reform, and without them reformation from social, civil, and moral evil is impossible.* Without the principles of Christianity, there is neither the element nor the power necessary to reform the world.

Further. Although reform principles may produce social progress, where they are urged and advocated without faith in Christ as a model or a motive, yet the result is only a temporary and a temporal good. What the world needs most is an *increase of benevolence, something that tends to destroy selfishness, and produce love to God and man.* Now, philosophy and religion say that *love only can beget love.* Every thing begets its kind. A selfish mind, by faith in Christ, becomes benevolent. Hence faith in Christ, as a manifestation of the love of God, is essential in order to motive power in the heart. Knowledge of truth is needful, but it is not the *one thing* needful in true reform. Those who have most knowledge are sometimes the worst men in the land. The thing wanted is love for men as a motive in the heart. We may know to do good, and have no disposition to do it. We want something within that empowers conscience, and actuates the will in accordance with the conviction of right. This power must likewise be a *love-power*—a power moving the affections. It must be a spiritual power, so that we shall seek the spiritual good as well as the temporal good of others. It must likewise be a God-begotten power in the soul, or our effort for men will not be to make them like God, by leading them to love and obey him. Mere conviction of right, without love for man, can be bribed; and there is a natural love of man that is mere instinct, more fully developed in some natures than in others. This has nature, not moral motive, for its basis, and is easily overcome by interest, and perverted by selfishness and passion. Hence what the soul wants most after a knowledge of duty, is a faith that works by love—a faith that causes the man to act out his convictions under the influence of the love-motive. Now we affirm that faith in Christ as the model and the motive, gives the soul this guide and this power. Reform without gospel faith may accomplish good, but it will be a good that is earthly and local in its nature, and that does not rise to the unselfish, the immortal, and the spiritual. God's love for man was revealed in Christ, and man's love for man is begotten by faith in Christ. Without this vitalizing faith, reform will be a mere struggle of natural benevolence against the predominating selfishness of the church and the world. *The struggle will promote self-righteousness on the one hand, and increase malignity on the other.*

But, more than all, the true Christian aims to bless all the interests of man. He looks upon man as an immortal being—as having a soul as well as a body. To emancipate a slave does not change his character nor reform his morals. To do good to men temporally is good—to do good to them temporally and spiritually is both better and best.

Freedom from sin is a greater blessing than freedom from slavery. The gospel aims to accomplish both. Reform, then, without Christianity, is but a partial, a temporal, and an imperfect good. The principle, the spirit, and the power of reform are combined in the gospel.

There may be activity in reform which is accompanied with a wrong spirit. *The denunciatory reformer would engage himself in the evil he denounces if his locality or circumstances were altered.* Some of the most self-elated, self-sufficient, and self seeking men that I have known, have belonged to this class of reformers. They labor for the right with a selfish and wrong spirit. They speak the truth in bitterness, and hence their truth becomes an occasion of hardening evil-doers, almost as much as the withholding or perverting of truth by the self-seeking and the unsanctified in the churches. The difference is, that truth, even though it be uttered in a bad spirit, will enlighten and awaken conscience in men—it will produce agitation, and hence ultimate benefit; while to pervert or withhold truth, is to refuse the only remedy which the Almighty prescribes for the evil of sin.

Let us have reform then—reform both in Church and State. Progress is the order both of the physical and the moral world. But we can have no permanent reform without the impulse and guidance of faith in Christ. The stability of reform must be conscience, and the impulse in reform must be love. But conscience and love are generated alone by faith in Christ. When the reformer moves in the sublimity of power, the momentum is generated in the heart.

Yours for the *right*, the *true*, and the *good*.

LETTER XII.

REFORMS AND REFORMERS.

MY DEAR SIR:—

Permit me now, in conclusion, to notice what I believe to be mistakes and mischiefs in the methods and opinions of Mr. Parker and his class of reformers.

No one doubts but that a great advance will yet be made in promoting equality and fraternity among men. There are abuses in the social usages of the world that need to be reformed; and the inquiry with the philanthropist and the Christian is, by what means can we best remove evil and promote good? Now, I for one, as you know, believe that but little good can be achieved by any one, no matter how good the intention may be, unless Christianity, *according to the orthodox interpretation*, be made the central and vital element in the effort.

Some years ago there was a mania abroad in the land in regard to associated labor; and many men of good intentions—men who really supposed that the highest good of themselves and others could be promoted by common-stock and common-labor communities — united themselves in associations formed more or less on the Fourier plan. Wise Christian men knew the experiments would fail; but it required a large number of experiments, and immense losses of property, and the wrecking of many families, to convince the friends of the scheme that it was impracticable for the ends they proposed to gain. Associations which receive the Christian faith as a bond of union have generally succeeded. Such were the common-stock associations of the early church of Christ; such are the Moravian associations, and others that might be named. But associations founded on selfish principles can not succeed. The motive inducing the effort is a self-destructive one. The members of such associations are drawn together, each one, by the motive to promote his own happiness and ease. Each individual seeks his own good as the supreme end, and uses the association as a means. Thus it is an aggregate of self-seeking minds. Every selfish effort strengthens the selfish principle in them, and an explosion in the end follows as a natural consequence. The Christian association seeks the good of the world by means of association. In their motive and labor the members seek to please Christ, not themselves. For this end they make self-denials, because they have a higher aim than self. They can find happiness in any labor which will promote the common object. Self is not supreme, but subordinate. With such motives association is possible, and generally profitable to the members, conducive to individual happiness, and to the glory of God.

All efforts of a philanthropic character should be encouraged up to the line of practicability and utility, *but ultra action produces re-action;* and there are many men of good intentions and enthusiastic minds who have little wisdom to judge either of human character or the feasibility of schemes to promote human good, who engage in popular reforms. The scheme of Christ includes the whole family of man. Its means are available and beneficent, and adapted to its end. It seeks to engage every individual both as a recipient and a disseminator of its blessings. It is pitiful to see those who evidently are not so wise as Christ, rejecting the divine scheme for a chimera of their own weak or wicked minds.

Christianity favors efforts that will benefit men temporally as well as spiritually. The Christian can labor with those who reject Christ, in schemes to promote the mere temporal good of men, provided there be nothing to hinder him from seeking in addition to this their highest good, by promoting that faith which alone gives peace and right motive in the soul. Most or all reforms that aim, in the estimation of worldly men, merely at the temporal good of men, are auxiliary to Christianity, and hence Christians should aid in promoting them, not only for temporal but ultimate good.

The land reform has beneficent phases. Monopoly of land is an injury and an evil. The system of Moses gave each family of each generation the privilege of accumulating, while yet it caused the fee of the soil to revert once in fifty years, thus preventing monopoly of soil by industrious parents for indolent children. This was the wisest and most comprehensive scheme possible. In our own country, at the beginning, something like this reversion law might have been adopted. And even now, while the rewards of industry should be sacredly protected, a policy should be adopted to prevent a monopoly of the *untilled soil* by men of capital. Let capital have its reward in other directions, but not by excluding actual cultivators of the land, nor by raising the prices of the virgin soil against those who desire to cultivate.

The vagaries of reformers who make no allowance for the different degrees of bodily or mental strength in individuals—who would give indolence the same reward as industry—who would give the wicked a bribe, and vice the means of indulgence, are contrary to nature, and injurious to good morals. Such vagaries are worse than weakness. Every plan that does not reward industry, calculation, and enterprise, is at war with virtue, and in league with vice. In this country, where all have equal chances, the prevention of monopolies is the main duty of those who seek to promote human welfare.

But in all associations, whether for reformation or for social protection and benefit, there is one central and universal defect which can be remedied only by Christianity.

The masonic institution, and other secret associations, may seek to some extent the moral and temporal good of their members, and of those connected with their members; but secret association gives men an advantage of their neighbors, if they are willing to take it. And beside, such associations are good or bad according to the character of their individual members. Where the general prevalence of Christianity has made the members better, lodges are better. Where the temperance reform banishes intoxicating drinks, lodges are sober. They are in themselves good or evil as Christian agencies from without the lodge have affected them.

Then there is still the central defect, a selfish motive. Providence has made a difference in the condition of men. Some are defective in body, in mind, in health. Some are laboring under evils by circumstances which society has induced. For these no selfish association can make provision. Christianity brings the influence of love, fraternity, and the authority of Christ to bear on its disciples, as motives to induce them to relieve those who, by providential arrangements, need relief, without respect of persons, of birth, or of sex. The most decrepid and needy are to be aided first, whether they be in one set of circumstances or another. *Christianity is the complement of Providence.* It is the system God has ordained to work into the inequalities of natural providence, and thus to balance natural evil by moral good. Provident associations of mechanics, or moral associations for the promotion of temperance and virtue, may be auxiliary to this great end; but Christianity alone, by church organization and by individual effort and beneficence, meets the imperfections of natural providences and balances them. Hence Christianity is a part of the divine economy of the world; and if its requirements were fully carried out, in act and spirit, there would be no evils to reform which would not be reached by human agency.

It is evident, then, that reformers, even if engaged in a good cause, are fools and blind in all cases, just so far as they reject the plan and the power offered by evangelical Christianity.

Those who seek to promote what are called "woman's rights," have a good object in view so far as they aim to promote equal legislation in relation to marital rights and parental duties. They pursue laudable objects when they seek to ameliorate the condition of female workers, and to advance wages in all cases in proportion to the value of the service. But when they labor to make women public speakers, or public actors in politics, or in any masculine endeavor, they are doing injury to society by acting against the constitution of nature and the revealed will of God.

The male is armed by nature for defense. He is strong to provide. He is voiced for public speech. The female is unarmed, and voiced only for social speech. A hen can crow, but it is ridiculous, and indicative of unmaternal qualities, when she does.

A woman, by an effort against nature, can give a public harangue, and can say things often more witty and beautiful than most men would say on the same subject. So some men could do certain domestic duties better than some women; but the change to accommodate the exceptions would be unnatural and unwise. There is no public speaking to be done that can not find advocates of the best talent among men; and the influence which social effort will produce for any cause in which a woman ought to be interested, will always be greater and better than any she could exercise by a public exhibition of herself. We say public exhibition of herself, because there are many persons who will go to see a woman speak in public, that attend to look at her person and gestures, and the flush of her excitement; and for no better purpose. Public places and speeches attract all sorts of characters. A woman may excite certain characters to applause which arises from a source that a chaste mind would abhor. Continued attention to work or office, every week for years, is of most value in all responsible labors. This married women could not give. Hence, male duties and wages, in such cases, is impossible.

The contention for the ballot is an indication of

like folly. The ballot is not given, as the common plea supposes, to represent property. If that were so, the rich would vote, as the slaveholders do, for their chattels. Every man who is a citizen has a ballot, whether he own property or not. Where the property of the country is represented in legislative bodies by those who have an equal interest with others, then every property-holder is represented whether they cast their ballot or not.

The incongruity to nature and circumstances of a woman's making speeches and voting is so palpable, that the evil can never gain much favor with the public. If all women were to vote, it would only double the number of votes, without increasing the strength of either side in civil questions, and if they had a ballot-box of their own, the Irish Catholic women would kill off our wives. In moral questions, the social influence of women to lead men to vote right is greater in the result than any thing that could be gained by antagonistic public action. Nature has made men the providers and the protectors, and has devolved duties upon a married woman that incapacitates her from providing, while it renders her necessarily the inmate of the home. The duties of most men require all days of the year in a steady employment. Nature forbids this ability to woman. A "woman's rights" lady might say to her like-minded sister, "Send your son John down this evening, and I will let my daughter Lucy go home with him after dark, to protect him from night rowdies;" but such a speech would be supremely ridiculous;—not more so, however, than the aims of Mr. Parker and others, who adopt the vagaries of foolish men and women in regard to what they call "woman's rights."

Let the women rule where only true happiness is found—in the home and social circle. Let the men, as nature requires, rule in public works, public assemblies, and out-door life. In families, as there can be only one will in relation to removals, expenditures, and many joint interests, if there be two opinions, after kind examination, which is seldom the case, then, as one will must govern in the case, the nature of things, in all ordinary instances, makes the husband's will supreme. If one or the other must yield, the husband is by the law of nature and revelation, the head of the family.

As we have stated, there is provision made against the possibility of much evil from the hallucinations of ultra reformers in this direction; but their effort repels many who desire to promote real reform. There are employments which women might fill—

there are trades which they might learn. In the practice of some branches of the medical profession women might do much good, and in some cases do it more appropriately than men. Let us not cease then to seek the good in this matter because of the vagaries of fools.

There is a class of reformers who are moved by their sympathies rather than by the reason and justice of the case. This class of men sometimes become dangerous to the well-being of society. They sympathize with scoundrels, and seek to save them from just penalties. They would make the penitentiary a place of comfortable retirement for villains; and thus induce such a state of things, that those who had never been there, would have no dread of the crime that would send them there; and those who had been there would be prepared for any villainy, if going back to light labor and comfortable quarters was the only consequence. To provide for the health and moral reform of criminals is proper, but to make their penalty a punishment is a duty, which it is crime against society to neglect.

The persons alluded to may be called instinctive reformers, becauses their impulses are organic, not moral. They frequently misdirect their compassion, because the impulse, in their case, is the highest law. But as subjection of the will to instinctive compassion is much better than subjection of the will to a corrupt public sentiment, hence the natural reformer may be a better man than a corrupt Christian teacher. But both are wrong in the main matter. There is the susceptibility of sympathy even in the lower animals. When one suffers, its cry will rally others of its class to the rescue. When the cry of distress is heard among animals, if one should take sides with the enemy that was crushing its suffering fellow, instead of rallying to the relief, it would be an apostate even from the best principles of brute nature. The "natural reformer" obeys the highest impulses of his nature—the professed Christian, who is not a reformer, has apostatized both from the higher impulses of humanity and from Christ. But the true Christian obeys Christ, *and by faith the higher instincts of humanity become rational and moral in their exercise.*

Let us apply these principles to some of the ultra notions of Mr. Parker and others. They speak of capital punishment, and denounce those who maintain the justice of the death penalty. They do this in common *ad captandum* phrase Now, while it is admitted that none but the willful and deliberate murderer should die, it can not be shown that the

Scriptures, or the principles of mercy guided by justice and reason, would permit the deliberate murderer to live. *Sympathy with the mere suffering of criminals is suspicious.*

Suppose I witness a pirate-ship attack a packet, and murder in cold blood the crew and passengers. I witness immediately after a revenue-cutter attack the pirate, and destroy the murderers of the innocent. There was as much of animal suffering in the one case as the other. But if I feel for the sufferings of the pirates as I do for the murdered passengers, I am a brute, possessing blind compassion without a sense of justice; or else I am a pirate at heart, sympathizing with like character.

It is painful to read the remarks of such reformers when they talk mawkishly about the momentary suffering of the murderer, while not a word is said, and apparently not an emotion felt, in view of the various, protracted, and excruciating sufferings which the villain may have inflicted upon his innocent victim.

It is an error to place the mercy of the New Testament in antagonism to capital punishment. The cardinal principles of the Christian Scriptures recognize the rectitude of the voluntary suffering of individuals, when it is necessary for the good of the whole, and of penal infliction when necessary as penalty for violated law. Even the death-penalty is recognized as proper when executed as a penalty. Paul says, "If I have done any thing worthy of death, I refuse not to die." Thus implying that such crimes were possible, and such penalty proper. The Mosaic institutions were for a peculiar people, in the initiatory stages of civilization and piety; but the Great Teacher sanctioned the death-penalty under the law of Moses, and thereby taught that taking life as a penalty is not wrong in itself. Hence the true inference is, that while it may be proper under the gospel to abate the death-penalty in all minor cases of crime, yet the infliction of the penalty on the part of society can never be shown to be wrong in itself. Jesus said to the Scribes and Pharisees who had abrogated the death-penalty in the case of the drunken, stubborn, and rebellious son that cursed his parents, and could not be reformed (Matt. xv.), "*God commanded, saying, Honor thy father and thy mother, and he that curseth father or mother let him die the death;* but ye say otherwise, and thus '*make the commandment of God of none effect.*'"

The ultimate principle, admitted by all, is, that as life is the highest individual good, it should be protected by the highest penalty. *If no other than the death-penalty will so certainly protect the life of the innocent, then those who would spare the life of the murderer, do it at the expense of the 'life of the innocent.* Now it has never been proved, and can not be, that imprisonment for life is a security against future murder by the condemned. A criminal was condemned by a jury to be hung for deliberate murder, in a neighboring State, a few years since. This penalty was commuted to imprisonment for life. In less than three years, he was pardoned; and for the crimes he has since since committed in Texas, the sympathizers with this murderer are guilty.

Commutation, or sentence to life imprisonment, endangers witnesses both before and after trial. A man of fifty commits a theft. He knows an imprisonment of ten years will follow the proof. Will he not thus be bribed to murder the witness? His penalty for both crimes can be no greater than that for the least; and if he murders the witness he hopes to escape. Will not the discontinuance of the death penalty transform most thieves into murderers? It has done so in many cases. If they commit the murder it is only imprisonment for a longer term, and that penalty doubtful; if they kill their victim, his testimony is impossible, and chances of escape are greater, while the penalty is in many cases no greater. Will it not take away from the public mind an impression of the sanctity of life, and thus in the estimation of villains decrease their sense of the guilt of murder? Michigan has been for some years the paradise of villains, owing, as all reason teaches, to the low estimate of guilt, and the light penalty of crime prevailing in that State. A virtuous community will punish the guilty. An immoral community will punish them by impulse, or not at all. The remission of the death-penalty has produced in Wisconsin, and is now producing in some other States, the most dreadful outrages. The conscience which God has given men says the murderer should die. This has been its testimony in all ages and in all time. When an *immoral philanthropy* remits the death-penalty, natural conscience is outraged, and men rise in mobs to inflict vengeance upon the murderer.

The pleas usually urged against the death-penalty have no real foundation either in morals or in reason. It is said that in some cases the innocent suffer death, and no remuneration can be made. So they may suffer imprisonment for life, and no remuneration can be made. Imperfection may attach to all law and penalty that is based upon testimony; but even this possible evil might be guarded against by sentence of imprisonment, without pardon, when doubt of the fact were possible.

It is said, again, that society, when it takes life for life, commits the same crime with the malefactor. Shame on such solecisms; then when we confine a murderer for life, we commit a crime equal in guilt to that of the criminal. When society takes a certain sum as penalty from a man who damaged his neighbor, it commits the same offense with the criminal, does it? If there were a society of devils for the promotion of crime, such arguments would receive a premium.

But life is sacred. It ought not to be taken in any case. It can be forfeited only to him who gave it. The statement is false in fact and in theory. If Mr. Parker were attacked by an assassin, with deadly weapons, and with the known intent to kill, it would be his duty to save his own life by taking the life of the murderer. Now, is not life forfeited as much after the act as before? It is certain that the guilt is as great, and that justice and universal conscience would affirm the same penalty after as before the fact.

It is said society is guilty in view of the imperfect

provision made for the moral and intellectual training of the masses of the people. If our school system be inadequate or partial, it should be reformed and strengthened; but this, while it would prevent the development of evil, in many cases would not prevent crime. It is a fallacy to argue that the absence of remedies used to prevent an evil is the cause of that evil. If the argument were true, all who have inadequate intellectual and moral training would be alike criminals; which statement is false and slanderous.

It is said, again, by the philosophers of the Fowler school, that the propensity to crime is organic; that criminal acts arise from the unbalanced impulsion of certain developments; and that therefore the criminal should be an object of pity rather than a subject for penalty. If this be true, then the Calvinistic system, which these reformers take pains to deride, is true in its utmost stringency. If this were true, then murderers should be exterminated for the same reason that we kill a viper or a tiger. Both are the *natural* enemies of human life; and reform in one case would be just as possible as in the other. The Chinese, who kill both the criminal and his children to prevent the propagation of crime, would be right. Such a philosophy ignores reform efforts of all kinds. Reform in that case would be possible only by knocking in the evil developments on the head with a hammer. The Fowler philosophy perpetrates the error of all superficial thinkers. It takes facts, true only as a general expression, and derives particulars from them. It likewise applies its principles wrong-end foremost. It makes development govern mind instead of urging the true application, that it is the character of the mind that produces the peculiarities of development in the body. The seed produces the tree—not the tree the seed. A bad spirit produces bad development. The law of creation and of philosophy agrees with the Scriptures that "every seed produces its own body, and '*so it will be in the resurrection.*'"

But it is argued that murderers dread imprisonment for life as much as they do the gallows. All facts, and all consciousness in all men, deny this assertion. If this be true, why do criminals and their friends seek a commutation of penalty? Why do all murderers joyfully accept commutation? Even the devil concedes the falsehood of this statement when he said, "All that a man hath will he give for his life."

Penalty is designed to prevent as well as to punish crime. The death-penalty is the highest restraint that can possibly be opposed to murder. Murder is unlike all other crimes. It is the crime of crimes: but it can never be distinguished as such without inflicting upon the murderer the highest penalty. By the death-penalty the murderer is taught to value the life of others as he does his own. *This is the golden rule.* And unless death be the penalty, a villain meditating crime can never value the life of another as he does his own. By the imprisonment-penalty he is taught to value the life of his neighbor as little as he values imprisonment in the penitentiary. Who dares to teach murderers this low estimate of life?

It is said that facts and statistics prove that imprisonment is a remedy as effectual in preventing murder as the death-penalty. This is not proved; and I believe it is not true. Facts, as far as they go, prove the contrary. The instances alleged in favor of abolishing the death-penalty, those of Catharine of Russia and the government of Tuscany, were of too short duration to prove any thing. On the other side, we have the case in the German States, where the statistics are accurate, and sufficient time for a fair experiment has been allowed. The "Conversation-Lexicon," a work of the highest authority concerning German topics, says, "Those States where, from a one-sided benevolence, the government wished to abolish capital punishment, were compelled again to avail themselves of it, and that on the ground that in the opinion of men death is the greatest of evils, in preference to which they would willingly undergo the most laborious life, with some hopes of escape from it, because the death-penalty is the most terrible of penalties."

Wordsworth, a man of the most highly-endowed intellect, the purest and the warmest benevolence, in the *London Quarterly Review*, No. 137, says: "Whenever it appears to be good for mankind, according to the arrangements of Providence, that death should be inflicted by human ministration, it is a *false humility*, a *false humanity*, and a *false piety*, for a man to refuse to be the instrument."*

Robespierre resigned his office in early life rather than sign a warrant for the execution of a criminal. His future life showed him to be a monster destitute by nature of the sense of justice.

The following passage in Blackstone (Book IV. chap. i.) should not be forgotten: "In France the punishment of robbery, either with or without murder, is the same; hence it is that though perhaps

* See Cheever on Capital Punishment.

they are subject to fewer robberies, *yet they never rob but they also murder*. In China murderers are cut to pieces, but robbers not; hence in that country they *never murder on the highway*, though they often rob." Is not this satisfactory proof that the man, or the legislature, that, through sympathy with criminals, aids to abolish the death-penalty, thereby stimulates villains to murder the innocent.

If this is not sufficient, take a fact nearer home. Capital punishment was abolished several years since in Michigan. The grand jury of Wayne County in that State made a presentment to the legislature, in which they say: "Facts, we are informed, have occurred in our midst, proving that some of the murderers in this county have been influenced and urged forward to their deeds of wickedness through the consideration that the death-penalty has been abolished from our penal code."

Much might be added, showing that in some cases imprisonment for life is a bribe to commit murder; in other cases it is no penalty, and in all cases it places the murderer where no further penalty for crime is possible. He may murder his keeper; he may poison the prison well, and thus murder all the inmates; his life is sacred, and he is above law; no further penalty can be inflicted.

That paragraph of your letter which is designed to have a point touched with sarcasm, which alludes to the repentance of murderers and the hanging of Christians, is to be regretted. The Bible nowhere teaches that willful murderers ever exercise repentance unto life. "No murderer hath eternal life abiding in him." That murderers repent, no one doubts. Judas repented and went to "his own place." Repentance is either selfish or holy. If it is repentance in view of the consequence to one's self, it produces remorse, or deceives the mind. Every criminal repents when the hand of the sheriff is on his shoulder. This is forced repentance. It is the murderer's repentance. It is honest repentance. But it is "repentance unto death." Not holy repentance, produced by faith in Christ.

Some I know believe that true repentance in such cases is possible. *If it be possible, the death-penalty is much more likely to produce repentance than the penalty of imprisonment.* Dr. Webster, while there was hope of escape or commutation, maintained the falsehood that he was innocent. When sentence was passed, and pardon or commutation denied, he became penitent and truthful. In "Bemis' Report," in Webster's last conversation with the sheriff he says: "All the proceedings in my case have been just. The court have discharged their duty. The law officers of the commonwealth did their duty, and no more. The verdict of the jury was just. The sentence of the court was just; *and it is just that I should die on the scaffold, in accordance with that sentence.*" Thus does the sentence of death, when there is no hope of escape, produce in some cases honest repentance. In Webster's statement that his sentence was just, and that he deserved to die, we have the same evidence given in many other cases when the crime is confessed. It is the decision of the human conscience, one which ought not to be violated, that the man who deliberately takes the life of his neighbor forfeits his own. The man who refuses to award this highest penalty to the highest crime manifests a corrupted sympathy, rejects the decisions of an honest conscience, and the conviction of human reason in all ages, and strengthens the hands of the guilty against the innocent.

Yours truly.

We have now traveled over the Philosophical, the Theological, and Reform vagaries of Theodore Parker, and have occasionally referred to others who are affiliated with the abnormal moral movements of our times. We have endeavored to separate the pure from the vile, and to reject nothing good, while we repudiated the evil. Perhaps we have, in our desire to grant all that charity demanded, allowed some things to stand as truth which the better-informed may condemn as error. We have done what we could. To God and sincere inquirers we commend the effort.

LETTER XIII.

WRITTEN REVELATION A NECESSITY IN ORDER TO THE MORAL DEVELOPMENT AND MORAL PROGRESS OF MANKIND.

MY DEAR SIR :—

You express a doubt whether there be any Revelation as I understand that word, and invite a statement of "*reasons.*" Health will scarcely permit me to pursue this correspondence, yet the hopes awakened by your last note encourage me to give "reasons for the faith that is in me."

I think it was the son of Sirach who said that "all things are set over against each other." A wiser than either Sirach or his son says, "Man was not made for the Sabbath, but the Sabbath for man."

There is a collocation of the providences of God with the developments of human life ; and there is an adjustment of moral appliances and means to human faculties, in order to produce the progressive development of the human family. Wherever any distinct adaptation in the universal fitness of things, is seen to be harmonious with other adjustments and perfect in itself, the conclusion is infallible that it is a part of that "stupendous whole" "whose builder and maker is God."

Now, Mr. Parker will no doubt admit the validity of this principle as applied to the natural world; but he will deny that the Bible is of God, and that its dispensations have an adaptation to the moral progress of mankind.

With Mr. Parker and his class of thinkers, reason and conscience are the highest guides of men; with the Christian, reason when enlightened by divine revelation, and conscience when empowered by divine authority, unite in the guidance of men.

Now, in my opinion this question can be settled. It can be shown that the Christian is right, and that the Bible is a necessary means in order to the development of man as an individual, and of mankind as a family.

We inquire, then, is the Bible of God? Was it made for man?

Let me premise that in the remarks which follow I do not propose to discuss any question concerning discrepancies in the Old Testament. There may be historical discrepancies and interpolations—there may be fables added in some of the minor books to the proper matter of revelation—there may be books in the canon whose places are not rightly adjusted. These questions we leave to the learned. Men of sense will inquire concerning the only thing that is of vital interest to them, i. e., Was the dispensation given by Moses revealed by divine authority to the Jews? and is the Christian dispensation a perfect, ultimate, and obligatory dispensation from God designed for all mankind, "to be manifested [*to all*] *in due time?*"

In speaking of the Old Testament as revealed to and for the Jews, we do not hence infer that as Christians we have no moral connections with the introductory dispensation. My views of this connection you have read, and the Christian public, on both sides of the sea, have approved, in the volume referred to. I make the preceding suggestions, only that your mind may be separated from some things which seem to trouble you, but which are not of importance in connection with our present inquiries.

Mr. Parker, and the skeptics generally, hold that reason—including intuitional and reflective reason—is a sufficient guide for men in matters relating to God. We can not see how men who are conversant with human history, some of whom have made philosophy a study, can adopt such an opinion. The highest result that reason can give on this subject has been worked out in such a variety of circumstances, that a man who fails to learn a lesson that all experience teaches, must have a will over which reason has, in some measure, lost its influence.

The testimony of universal experience is, that all men have an idea of the *existence* of God. But men can not have an intuition of the *character* of God, for the plain reason that a knowledge of character implies comparison, quality, and hence requires a *process* of reason. It is a shallow fallacy in philosophy, that Mr. Parker should assume, as he does, that men have an innate idea of the character as well as the being of God. The moral duties of men to each other may be learned in a good measure by experience, even up to the measure of the golden rule. I know the effect which the conduct of another has upon myself. I judge of that conduct, whether it is in itself right or wrong; and hence, by this process, I can determine what would be right in my neighbor's case, were our circumstances changed. Reason is clouded in men, and it is developed slowly in nations; hence, while rules of human morality may be developed by reason, yet it is only in the best ages and in the highest minds that these higher moral conceptions have appeared. But the character of God and the duties of man to his Maker, are different things. Man without faith has no immediate experience of the divine character, and having a mixed experience by Providence, it is absolutely impossible for reason to clothe the idea of God with the moral attributes which belong to the divine nature.

Now, the universal experience of nations and races of men has certified these facts. The highest attainment of reason in relation to God has been skepticism, or diversity. This was the result in India, in Greece, in Rome, in France, in Germany, and in America. In all ages and nations which have furnished an opportunity for the ultimate development of the reason, the results have been the same.

Greece gathered all the gods of all nations into her capital city. This was the ultimatum of human reason, in the direction of variety. Her philosophers believed in a divine being; but, while they doubted of all the idolatries of the people, they differed as much among themselves as the people did in relation to prevalent superstitions. Such was also the development in Rome. Tully and others expressed the ultimatum of reason in the affirmation, that all things in relation to the gods and the future world were matters of doubt.

Reason reached the same ultimatum in France and Germany. Revelation in those countries was either forbidden or perverted. The people followed the prevailing superstition, while the philosophers reached a skepticism that was malignant and terrible in its effects on human character and human happiness; so terrible, that the people who had been seduced by it, were glad to take refuge again in the stronghold of the old superstition, as the least of two evils.

The highest result that reason could attain, unaided by revelation, and aided by all the light and experience of past ages, was wrought out fairly in France. It was a complete triumph of skepticism. Every thing concerning God, and man, and the future was involved in utter doubt. Reason triumphed, and ultimated in the worship of herself, in the form of a profligate woman. Reason even doubted her own affirmations; and only enough of light was left to see the darkness into which she had plunged.

This the best minds of the age stated, in words full of true and solemn portent—words which should teach others to recede from the abyss into which these skeptical philosophers looked before they fell.*

In Great Britain and America skepticism can not

* Diderot, dying after a life of doubt and disappointment, said to friends that stood by his couch to close his eyes in the last sleep, "I am about to take a leap in the dark."

The justly-celebrated Rousseau uttered a striking description of the results of skepticism, and the moral character and aim of skeptics. It is true to life, and true for all time—a picture of the highest product of reason unaided by revelation.

He said:

"I have consulted our philosophers, I have perused their books, I have examined their several opinions. I have found them all proud, positive, and dogmatizing, even in their pretended skepticism, knowing every thing, proving nothing, and ridiculing one another; and this is the only point in which they concur, and in which they are right. Daring when they attack, they defend themselves without vigor. If you consider their arguments, they have none but for destruction; if you count their number, each one is reduced to himself; they never unite but to dispute; to listen to them was not the way to relieve myself from my doubts. I conceive that the insufficiency of the human understanding was the first cause of this prodigious diversity of sentiment, and that pride was the second. If our philosophers were able to discover truth, which of them would interest himself about it? Each of them knows that his system is not better established than the others; but he supports it because it is his own: there is not one among them who, coming to distinguish truth from falsehood, would not prefer his own error to the truth that is discovered by another. Where is the philosopher who, for his own glory, would not willingly deceive the whole human race? Where is he who, in the secret of his heart, proposes any other object than his own distinction? Provided he can but raise himself above the commonalty, provided he can eclipse his competitor, he has reached the summit of his ambition. The great thing for him is to think differently from other people. Among believers he is an atheist, among atheists a believer. Shun, become so prevalent, because in these countries Christianity is better understood; and where it does prevail, it will seek to attach to itself many of the virtues which Christianity has introduced: but the result of the unguided reason can in no circumstances be any thing better than doubt, varied in its form by the diversity of the different minds that propagate it. Which one of the English skeptics agreed with another in respect to the character of God or human duty?* Who agrees with Theodore Parker or Joseph Barker in America? No one ever did or ever can. Skeptics agree in doubt, but they can not agree concerning the things about which they doubt. The effort to propound any

shun then those who, under pretense of explaining nature, sow in the hearts of men the most dispiriting doctrines, whose skepticism is far more affirmative and dogmatical than the decided tone of their adversaries. Under pretense of being themselves the only people enlightened, they imperiously subject us to their magisterial decisions, and would fain palm upon us for the true causes of things the unintelligible systems they have erected in their own heads; while they overturn, destroy, and trample under foot all that mankind reveres, snatch from the afflicted the only comfort left them in their misery, from the rich and great the only curb that can restrain their passions; tear from the heart all remorse of vice, all hopes of virtue, and still boast themselves the benefactors of mankind. 'Truth,' they say, 'is never hurtful to man.' I believe that as well as they, and the same, in my opinion, is a proof that what they teach is not the truth."

* See Leland and Gregory.

thing positive is, in all cases, a failure; and in most cases—as in Priestley's form of worship and Parker's philosophy of God—the effort is ridiculous as it is futile. The wandering mind feels the need of something positive in religion; and having rejected revealed truth, it seeks to attain from reason such baseless dogmas as Parker's "idea, sense, and conception of God." The mind of man was made to rest in faith; and when skepticism deprives men of this support, the soul feels more of unrest and deprivation than do the heathen, who rest in a false faith. Unaided reason can doubt, but it can not affirm any thing in relation to God and the future that will satisfy the soul.

Man was not made to be the victim of skepticism. Heathenism is better than this, just as ignorance is better than aberration. Revelation was made for man; made to elevate the races progressively, from a state of nature to a state of grace; made to spread from families to nations, and finally to reach all mankind.

But leaving strictures on doubt and negation, which are to positive religion as night is to the day, let us look at some thoughts which may prepare us more intelligently to consider the positive side of the argument, which maintains that the Christian

Scriptures are a revelation from God, containing the ultimate rule of faith and duty.

All things are progressive in their development. Individually or socially considered, in the life-history of things there is an infancy, youth, and maturity. "First the blade, then the ear, then the full corn in the ear." The Scriptures affirm this principle. The family of man are, as a family, subject to this law. There are ages of infancy, of youth or tuition, and of maturity. The first law would be one relating to animal wants, and adapted to the period of childhood. Hence the law, "Thou shalt not eat forbidden fruit," and those of similar character. Hence the name of God as *Al-Shaddi*, God of Power, or God of Nature, as known to the patriarchs.

The second dispensation would be adapted to man's tuition in the next stage of development. Hence the Mosaic: which, as pictures in a child's primer, with explanations attached; and a written moral law in the briefest form, gave to man a more perfect idea of God and of moral duties.

The third stage would be the ultimate and perfect—"the full corn in the ear."

The first stage, or patriarchal, would develop itself from the family into a nation; the second from the nation to all nations.

Men of the Christian age, together with the knowledge of their own dispensation, get the knowledge generated and transmitted by the two preceding ones. The foundation-principles of these were developed into the final and perfect form of Christianity.

The vital importance of the *family*—especially its law of duty and obedience—is developed fully in tho first dispensation. Abraham is chosen because he will instruct and command his children (Gen. xviii. 19). In all ages of revelation this important principle needed to be understood. Families trained to obey righteous authority, and having their consciences and hearts nurtured by the admonition and fear of God, are the anchor-hope of a free state.

Man needs to know also the relation of a state, as a whole, to the divine government; that every state has its probation; that departure from righteous principle will, in the end, bring dissolution and disaster. This is the teaching of the national history of Israel. It exhibits to all ages the principles upon which God administers his govermnent over favored nations, and the discipline which they must incur for national offenses against justice and mercy.

These three stages of development are likewise exhibited in individuals. There is first the animal, when animal appetite governs. Second, the intellectual period of growth, when law and penalty governs. Third (for those who rise to it), a dispensation of love and fruit-bearing, when faith governs.

There are likewise the lineaments of these three stages in the advance of each individual that enters the kingdom of heaven on earth. An illustration is furnished in the experience of Paul. Before he became a Jew spiritually, i. e., before he apprehended the law as being from God, and obligatory upon his mind, he was free from a sense of sin; he was sensual, governed by his own natural impulses. Second, when he realized the spirituality of the law, he became a true Pharisee; felt condemned for sin; and endeavored to escape condemnation by works of law. Third, he was made free by faith; and that which before was a work of the intellect and will, without inward love and impulse, now became easy and holy, being prompted by love which was produced by faith in Christ. Through this process, in some degree, passes every individual who rises *from nature through conviction into grace.*

Hence also the three developments of the name of Jehovah. *Al-Shaddai*, God of nature or of power. Second, *Jehovah*. A development of the same name known to the fathers (Ex. vi. 3); but, in the second dispensation, to be changed from Al-Shaddai to Jehovah, who now developed himself in moral law and tuition. In the third, *Father*, *Son*, and *Holy Spirit*—the God of power, and developed by law and tuition into the God of grace. Thus by the progressive development of the divine character, has the human mind been raised through the first and second, into the third and ultimate state of knowledge.

With these preliminary remarks, I invite your attention to the following train of thought, as proof of the *Necessity of a Written Revelation.*

I have in my published volumes discussed the details of the statements which follow. An outline view will indicate the course of thought which you will find more fully and carefully stated in the volumes which I send you.

Every species of nature may be cultivated. Its properties or faculties may be improved. This is true in a general sense; and especially true as we rise toward the higher species. But the improvement of any species must come from one higher than itself. There may be choice individuals produced by chance circumstances, but *no species can raise itself* above its natural level.

Now, a distinguishing characteristic of man is, that he is both a *cultivable* and a *cultivating* being. He cultivates the species of nature fitted to his use, while he himself is capable of moral culture.

But as it requires man's superior powers of intellect and example to cultivate the orders below him, and raise them above their natural condition, so it requires the powers of a being above man to elevate him, as a moral being, into a new sphere of thought and feeling. The conclusion, therefore, arises not only from the *analogy* but from the *necessity* of things, that man cultivates nature, and Christ cultivates man.

But what are the means of culture *adapted* to man's nature as a moral being? There are four, namely, *written language*, *faith*, *conscience*, and *example.* Faith and conscience are subjective susceptibilities, and written language and example are objective means *answering to them;* And by the interaction of these, man may be cultivated into the sphere of a superior species. But the external means must be exercised by an agency superior to himself, or he will never rise above his natural selfish and earthly nature.

Notice the facts and their application. Written, or sign-language, is generally supposed to be a natural product of the human reason. However this may be, it is certain that men, after they have attained a settled social condition, always form for themselves a language of signs. Without this they can not ascend from the first stages of barbarism. Fixed signs of thought are necessary before there can be commercial progress, forms of law, or fixed moral principles.

Sign-language is one of the distinguishing characteristics of the human species. Animals below man can communicate to each other certain ideas, but they can not impress upon external objects, and thus transmit to others, a fixed sign of their thought.

If, then, sign-language is a characteristic of man, and if he can not be elevated from barbarism to social and civil position without it, it would be absurd to suppose that his moral culture can be accomplished without this necessary medium.

Hence, so soon as the primitive nations became settled, and so soon as sign-languages were matured, God gave to man, in order to his moral progress, a written record of the past—of his character, and of his will; and these, together with new and progressive spiritual ideas generated by forms and external types, were rendered permanent in sign-language, and transmitted to the future by the ritual dispensation of Moses.

The second characteristic which distinguishes man from irrational beings, is faith. Animals receive their knowledge through the senses; man receives most of his knowledge by credence.* All the experience of the past is given to him by faith in testimony. It is faith alone that connects man with the past and the future—with God and the spiritual world. Faith depends on written language to reach the past, and on hope to reach the future, and on written revelation to know God. Man is a believing being by creation; and without faith he is no better than the brute—with a bad faith he is worse.

Faith is the spiritual sense. By it spiritual objects become subjective in the soul, as external physical objects become subjective by sense. By faith in revealed truth, the character of God becomes a conscious entity in the soul. "Faith works by love." "He that loveth knoweth God, for God is love." Thus by faith the character of God, and the life and precepts of God recorded in divine reve-

* There is a class of philosophers who contend that they receive all their knowledge through the senses. By this method men may approximate animal natures; but the distinguishing characteristic between sense and spirit can never be entirely obliterated.

lation, become united in the moral culture of man. In this way the subjective susceptibility of faith is met by the objective actuality of divine revelation.

Mark, now, that without divine truth externally revealed, the susceptibility of faith is injurious and evil to man. Faith controls man's character and his life. If I believe my neighbor to be a bad man, I will feel as though he were so. If a Catholic believes he ought to confess to the Virgin Mary, his conscience will reprove him if he does not do so. Faith forms man's character and his conscience in accordance with what the man believes, whether that be true or false. Faith of itself is blind; it needs a guide as much as a blind man needs eyes. Without revealed religion as the guide of faith, "the blind lead the blind, and both fall into the ditch."

But faith is connected with conscience as well as with sign-language in the moral development of man. This brings us to the third fact in the means of human culture. There are two elements in efficient faith—one the external fact, the other the divine authority of the fact. Conscience will respond to no truth unless faith delivers it as coming from God. Great souls, such as Plato, Seneca, and Tully, have spoken great truths; but who cared for these? None but those who did not need them. These were men like others—liable to mistakes—could give only their *opinions*—had no authority over men. Their sayings, therefore, could neither awaken or guide the conscience.

God has so constituted the soul, that conscience will enforce no truth upon the life with efficiency, unless it has God in it. The moment faith sees God in truth, that moment conscience awakes and enforces it as a duty. Jesus Christ himself did not teach that his truth would have full reforming efficacy until after his resurrection. He taught that by his resurrection and the advent of the Spirit, the evidence of divine authority would be given to his truth, and *then* it would attain new power and application in the souls of men. Truth alone has no power with the conscience. When truth comes in the name of God, then conscience awakes and enforces obedience.

But mark, now. Conscience, like faith, is blind without a guide, and with a blind guide it is doubly blind. If a man believe in no God, he will have no conscience in relation to any religious duty. If he believe his god sanctions theft, as do the devotees of Kalé, he will steal. If he believe his god sanctions child-sacrifice, conscience will enforce the murder, even against the parental instinct. So faith governs conscience, and both are false and foul without truth. With truth recognized as being only of human origin, faith is dead and conscience inefficient. Hence, the *truth*, and not only the truth, but *God-revealed truth—the truth of God* in *written language*—is the only true guide of the soul.

God has so constituted the soul that a written revelation is required in order to moral progress. As God is true, that revelation would be given. As God is true, that revelation *has been* given in the Christian Scriptures. A revelation of truth in progressive dispensations, up to the perfect in *love*, in *precept*, and in *example.*

We come now to the fourth requisite in order to the moral culture of man—a perfect example of human duty.

Theory is never perfect without example. Oliver Evans could not give his perfect theory of a steam-mill, and say to any one who understood his words and his plan, "Go and build a mill." His common-sense would teach him that the *practice* has to be learned as well as the theory. The master-workman must take the saw and hatchet, and *practice the theory in the presence of the pupil*, and put the learner through the routine of the labor. So in all things:

theory is only a part of knowledge; the practice has to be learned by example. So in religion. We needed not only the precept, but the example under the precept. This Christ has given. In the New Testament, Jesus is seen practicing the divine precept, and saying to his disciples, "Follow me."

Again, example is needed not only of moral duty, but of the spirit in which duty is to be discharged. This also is given in the New Testament.

Again, as precepts must be general in their nature, there are many specific applications of them which men could not know were it not for the example of Christ. When a son knows the character, and spirit, and motives of his father, he will be able to judge, *in his absence*, what his father would do in specific cases, and hence what he would have him do. So the example and spirit of Christ is a sure guide to his disciples in applying his precepts to the specific duties of life. When the believing mind inquires, what would Christ have me do in this case? the life and Spirit of Jesus, revealed in the Scriptures, will guide to the right conclusion.

But, finally, and above all, in order to man's continued progress toward the perfect, he needs an example that is ever above him—the example of one whose excellence will show him his defects, and whose love and proffered aid will invite him to higher attainments. Faith in Christ's example induces a sense of unworthiness, at the same time that faith in his sacrifice for us, moves the soul by love, and induces self-denial for others. *This is the true Christian consciousness*, and highest moral condition. (Matt. xi. 28–30.)

No one will doubt but that a sense of present imperfection and a struggle for higher attainment in holiness, is the method of moral progress. Now, at the entrance of the straight gate that leads to life stands the Saviour of men. He is ever before his disciples. The light of his perfect character shows them their defects. The love of his heart strengthens and encourages by the way. The mark of the prize of their high calling is to attain the perfection of his character; and to those who are running the race with whatever of knowledge and strength they possess, the divine favor and the divine providence are a conscious blessing and constant guard.

Thus, my dear sir, I think it is plain that the Bible was made for man; that it possesses the characteristics which are adapted to develop his moral faculties up to the perfect. A *revealed written* revelation is a necessity of man's moral nature. The Bible meets the necessity of the case, and therefore the Bible is of God. Yours truly.

LETTER XIV.

REVELATION THE MOTIVE-POWER IN HUMAN PROGRESS.

MY DEAR SIR:—

I did not purpose to trouble you with another letter; but your last note brings to view a point where I think you and many others have fallen into a grave misapprehension. That point is expressed in the paragraph quoted below. I will not open again the discussion in relation to those professing Christians whom you charge with complicity with sin. A word or two with reference to alleged Bible authority for slavery, and then I shall show—I hope conclusively—that the "facts" are not "against my logic," as you allege, but that they sustain, decisively, the views to which you seem to think they are opposed.

You say: "Almost thou persuadest me to believe a Written Revelation necessary. But I put facts against logic. How happens it, if the Bible be a book of revealed religion, that progressive movements are generally led by those who do not hold your views of the Bible? How happens it that reformers have to advance against the resistance and denouncements of the most influential churches, who often justify wrong by the Bible; as you know has been the case in the anti-slavery discussion in this country. It is true that while they defend slavery by the Bible, many of them profess to be opposed to slavery; but in this they are either hypocrites or accusers of their own book: for if the Bible (as I think it does) sanctions the practice of slaveholding, they ought to defend the institution. By condemning it, they condemn their own Scriptures."

Now, sir, I admit, as you know, to some extent, your allegation against the American churches; but I deny its application entirely to the true church of Christ. It has always been the few who, in the martyr ages of human progress, have stood and achieved the victory, both against church and state; but those few have stood in the light of the Bible, and have succeeded by the power of conscience strengthened by Bible faith. In relation to those who seek to sanction sin by the Bible, it proves nothing now, any more than it did in the time of the prophets, and of Christ. Neander, who, I believe, is held in high esteem by you, somewhere says that men interpret the Scriptures by their own hearts. This is a true saying. The moral disposition of a man will determine what use he will make of the Bible.

A certain kind of servitude was no doubt admitted by Moses. By the necessities of the Mosaic economy, the soil belonged to Israelites. The reversion land law returned the fee of the farms in Israel to the family of the original holder, at the end of each fifty years. Strangers, therefore, among the Jews, had to seek labor and subsistence as servants. Hence there was a life servitude, or a servitude until the Jubilee, but the Jubilee freed *all the inhabitants of the land.* Hence there could be no such thing (and there was no such thing) as an accumulation of slaves in Israel. Beside this, the mitigations of the law of Moses (and especially the law forbidding the return of fugitives) alleviated, even in the dispensation "which made nothing perfect," the fearful rigors of the slavery which existed in that age. A servant, being of the same color with his master, if he were misused, could escape to Israel or from Israel, and the "fugitive law" (the opposite of ours) forbade his return.

But the dispensation of Moses was inspired for

that age, and for the Jews. It was only a stage of progress toward the perfection of the gospel. He is either an ignorant man or a sinner, who endeavors to justify slavery under the gospel by any servitude which may have existed during the introductory dispensation. If slavery may thus be justified, so may polygamy. Beside, if the Bible tolerates slavery, it is the slavery of poor whites, not of negroes. Its servitude was predicated on condition, not color. Every man, therefore, who attempts to justify slavery by the Bible, should be held responsible for teaching that the enslavement of the poor is justified by the Scriptures.

There are those, I know, who justify American slavery by the New Testament. For such men, educated in the slave States, I could find an apology; but for northern Christians who hold such sentiments, argument is not the thing needed. In the divine government pardon or penalty is the issue with them.

They tell us that "Christ regulated slavery;" that "he gave precepts regulating the conduct of the master and the slave in their several relations." So he regulated assault and battery, and gave precepts that, when a man is smitten on the one cheek, he should turn the other. Has he, therefore, justified assault and battery? Christ abrogated slavery by the golden rule—by placing all men upon the platform of civil equality—by making it a fundamental tenet of his religion that those who had privileges should labor to elevate others up to their own position; and thus practically love their neighbor as themselves. Slavery is expressly abrogated in the epistle to Philemon, who is required to receive his old servant "*not now as a servant*," but as a brother man and a brother Christian. The 6th chapter of first Timothy you have translated rightly. The first verses teach as distinctly as any words can convey the same truth, that those servants who had "*believing masters*" were not "under the yoke" of slavery, as were those whose masters had not received the gospel. Those who had not believing masters are exhorted to endure their affliction for Christ's sake; and those who had "*believing masters*" are exhorted (as emancipated slaves are in the West Indies) still to labor for their old masters, rather than for another; because their master was "now a *brother*;" and as the *benefit* of their labor had to be given to some one, it was a Christian duty to prefer that the believing master should receive that benefit.

If they were still considered slaves in the legal

sense, such an exhortation to the two different classes would be absurd. Those who had believing masters were evidently no longer held "under the yoke" of involuntary servitude.

But let us pass to the main and ultimate question as to the facts. Has not the Bible given impulse and direction in every successful effort that has ever been made for the moral progress of mankind? Let us see whether "the facts are against my logic."

The Bible itself, as you know, claims that its mission is to enlighten the world, and to advance the moral interests of the human family. As this is a Bible topic, I can do no better than remodel for you a discourse recently delivered upon this particular subject. I ask your attention to the discriminations which it makes, and to the facts by which the conclusion is reached. We have shown, as we think, that human nature is so constituted, that revealed religion is necessary in order to the moral development of our race. Do historical facts verify this conclusion?

We have said that the Bible claims to be both light and power in the moral progress of the world. I wish you would observe this, because in some of your letters you speak of the orthodox party claiming more for the Bible than it claims for itself. This may be true when some eulogists of revelation claim for it extraordinary excellences of style, and other extrinsic matters of that sort. But it is not true in regard to the claim of moral light and power. *The Bible does claim these, and all friends of revelation should claim them for it.* Notice this.

The Old Testament writers speak of their own dispensation as the light of *their* age; and the minds of the old prophets glow with inspiration when they refer to the increased light and purity of Messiah's age—an age when "the light of the moon was to be as the light of the sun, and the sun itself would shine with sevenfold effulgence." "To the people that sat in darkness and in the valley and the shadow of death," they declared that a "light would spring up." About the last utterance of the last of the prophets refers to the purifying power of the Messiah's dispensation, and to the spiritual light which would be revealed in his day. (Mal. iii. 1, 2,) "Behold I will send my messenger before me [John Baptist], and he shall prepare the way before me; and the Lord [Messiah] whom ye seek shall suddenly come to his temple; even the messenger of the covenant whom ye delight in: behold! he shall come, saith the Lord of hosts! (2) But who may abide the day of his coming? and who shall stand when he appeareth? For he shall be like a *refiner's fire* and like *fuller's soap;* and he shall sit as a *refiner and purifier af silver.*" That is, the Messiah's dispensation would purify and elevate those who were subjects of its influence. And (ch. iv. 2, 3) while the wicked would be condemned and destroyed, "to those who feared the Lord the Sun of righteousness would arise with healing in his beams."

To this light of the old dispensation the people who first heard the gospel, and who lived in the transition period (from the death of Christ to the fall of Jerusalem) were exhorted to take heed. Although it shone in a darker dispensation, yet it was a "lamp" in the path that led to a fuller manifestation of divine love and truth. This view of the relations of the Old and New Testament light the Apostle Peter beautifully expresses in his second letter, chap. i. 19, "We have also a more sure word of prophecy, whereunto ye do well that ye take heed, as unto a light that shineth in a dark place [age], UNTIL the day dawn, and the day-star [of the gospel dispensation] arise in your hearts." The Old Testament dispensation—as interpreted by the inspired prophets—was as a light in the night. The

New Dispensation was daylight, which was then dawning in the hearts of believers.

John Baptist, the forerunner of Jesus, who came to reprove his nation and to call them to repentance, as the proper preparation for the reign of Messiah, was called "a burning and a shining light." The first prophetic announcement of the character of Jesus, after his advent, by the pious Simeon, was that he should be "a light to enlighten *the Gentiles*, and the glory of his people Israel," and that he would "be set for the fall [by repentance] and rising again [to a higher moral state] of many in Israel." That is, the Gentile nations should be enlightened by Christ, and "many" of the Jewish nation would feel condemned in the light of his dispensation, and would rise again into the higher moral condition which it required.

John, although himself called a light, affirmed that he was not *that light* which was to raise a portion of the Jewish people, and enlighten the Gentile nations. "He was not that light, but was sent to bear witness of that light"—"that was the true light that enlighteneth every man that cometh into the world," both Jew and Gentile.

Jesus himself claimed to be "the light of the world." "I am," said he, "come a light into the world, that whosoever believeth in me should not abide in darkness." "I am the light of the world; he that followeth me shall not walk in darkness, but shall have the light of life." The truth which he declared as the basis of condemnation was, that "light had come into the world, and men loved the darkness rather than the light, because their deeds were evil."

The apostles apprehended distinctly that the increased light of revelation was the reforming and the elevating power of the nations. They not only understood the fact, that revelation was the moral life and light of men, but they understood the relations of this fact, and its place in the moral progress of the world. "The darkness," said they, "is past, and the *true light* now shineth." They speak of the church of Christ as "the light of the world," and Christians as "the children of the light." There is, probably, no other topic which suggests illustrations to the minds of the sacred writers more varied and beautiful than this one; and there is none other which conveys to us truth of more vital importance. There is, in my opinion, no figures in human language more striking than those which the inspired writers use in presenting truth under the symbol of light, not only in the past and present, but in the apocalyptic visions of the future. What can be more striking than the figures of the revelator. Forecasting the period of the Reformation, he speaks of the "two witnesses," the Old and New Testaments, which, clothed in sackcloth, were lying without vitality in the streets—these are elevated into the heavens, from which position they attract the attention of men, and send the rays of the Reformation down into their hearts. The church of Christ, witnessing for truth, is spoken of as "A woman, clothed with the *sun*, and the *moon* under her feet, and upon her head a crown of twelve *stars*."

But I need not to dwell upon the fact that the Scriptures *do* claim that the truth of revelation is the moral light of the world. There is another fact connected with this subject; one which the cursory reader overlooks; but it is one which relates to the vital power of truth—the Scriptures claim that there is spirit and life in the truth which they reveal. To this *life of the light* I ask your attention before the historical analysis which is to follow. It is well to ascertain accurately the apostolic conception, and the breadth of the Scripture claim, before an appeal to external testimony.

To see an evil is one thing; to lead men to feel

the turpitude of evil, in itself, in themselves, and in the sight of God, is quite another thing. We have noticed this fact in a previous letter. It will not be necessary to dwell on it here. Suffice it to say, that in order to the moral progress of men two things are necessary. First, that men should *see* the evil; and second, that they should *feel* such a sense of the evil as will lead them to turn from it, and seek a higher life. Light is necessary to see the evil. A sense of God and duty with that light, is necessary to lead men from the evils which the light reveals.

Now, this *reproving* or *convicting* power accompanies the light of revealed religion. There may be intellectual culture where there is no moral purity. The first benefit is scarcely a blessing without the last. A knowledge of right and duty only renders one a greater hypocrite unless he have moral sense and moral life sufficient to conform to his own convictions. Now, this *reproving* power, which leads men to feel the evil of sins which they perceive, the Scriptures claim for themselves as a spiritual efficacy which accompanies revealed truth. Let us notice and illustrate this fact.

We have shown elsewhere that truth has power over the moral nature of men, only so far as a sense of God and duty is in it. There needs to be *life* as well as *light* in that truth which has reforming power in the world. This *life-power* the sacred writers claim as belonging to the gospel. It is a power by which men feel reproved or condemned for the sins which truth reveals to them—a power which leads them to reprove evils in themselves and others "made manifest by the light."

Christ is spoken of as being not only the "light," but the "life" of men. The second Adam gave not only light to the intellect, but life to the heart. He was a "life-giving" as well as a "light giving" Spirit. "The words that I speak unto you," said Jesus, "they are spirit and they are life." "I am the light of the world. He that followeth me shall not walk in darkness, but shall have the *light of life.*" "I am the way, the truth, and the *life.*" Now, this life, or reproving, or convicting power, is the glory of the gospel. Without this, the intellect may be enlightened, while the conscience will be dead and the heart corrupt. Hence Jesus said, "Ye will not come unto me lest your deeds should be reproved." The one thing needful, after the understanding is enlightened in relation to moral duties, is this reproving life in the conscience of men, which produces "repentance unto life." *The*

Holy Ghost is personally this reproving power. The divine Spirit gives life to the soul, by the truth. Christ taught that when the Comforter, which is the Holy Ghost, should come into the world, "He would persuade—reprove—the world of sin, righteousness, and judgment."

The disciples understood that without this moral power, the mere intellectual light of truth would increase sin instead of producing holiness. Hence they said, "Christ hath made us ministers of the New Testament: not of the letter, but of the spirit; for the letter killeth, but the spirit giveth life." Paul, in his letter to the Christians at Ephesus, states with great distinctness the effect and the necessity of gospel truth, both as an enlightening and reproving power. (v. 13) "All things that are reproved are made manifest by the light; for whatsoever doth make manifest is light: wherefore [the gospel] saith, Awake, thou that sleepest, and arise from the dead, and Christ shall give thee light." That is, the light of revealed religion shows the moral evils which exist in the heart and in the world; and the life-power of the Spirit accompanying that light, leads us to feel the guilt of these evils.

Notice, now, an instance of the influence and

practical operation of this moral power of truth, as it effected the reformation of the world in the apostolic age. The same principle we shall see is applicable in all other cases, and in all time.

Take the case of the city of Ephesus, to the Christian inhabitants of which Paul writes the passage we have quoted. The apostle describes this city as sitting in darkness, and her citizens as corrupted by the practice of the most debasing vices. He says to the Christians, "Ye were sometime darkness, but now are ye light in the Lord. Walk as children of the light, and have no fellowship with the unfruitful works of darkness, but rather reprove them; for it is a shame even to speak of those things which are done of them in secret." Such was the celebrated city of Ephesus when the light and reproving power of the gospel reached her. What was necessary in her case?

Intellectual light was not what the men of Ephesus wanted. They lived in the Augustan age, the noon-day of ancient civilization. They lived when the light of reason had reached its meridian in the ancient world. They lived in the Eclectic age, when the best thoughts were collected from Plato and all the great thinkers that had gone before. It was the age of Seneca and Pliny, of Tacitus, Josephus, and Plutarch, the crowning authors of the ancient literature, in morals, history, science, and religion.

And this city of Ephesus was one of the points in Asia where art and letters had done all they could do for human culture. Diana of the Ephesians was one of the purest shrines at which the old world worshiped; and her temple was one of the most magnificent structures that was ever erected and adorned by human hands. About the time that Paul wrote the passage which we have quoted, describing the appalling corruption which prevailed in the city, Pliny, one of the wisest and most refined men of his age, speaks of Ephesus as "one of the luminaries of Asia." The one considered her as full of light, the other looked upon her as full of darkness. Both views were true, according to the standard by which the writers formed their judgment. Pliny saw her as the seat of the best civilization and the highest culture that a people without revelation had ever attained. But underneath the glare of vain-glory, Paul saw a degree of corruption that defiled her very heart. She was "a whited sepulcher, full of dead men's bones." The light that was in her was darkness. Those who lived in it said, "Behold, we see!" and the baptism of their sacred rites, by which they sought to purify themselves, only infected them with baser pollution.

What was needed, now, in order to reform and save this people? Was it civilization? This they had attained in the highest degree. Was it philosophy? Some of the most celebrated schools were in this city. Was it perfection of art? The best models of the age, some of which still exist as artistic wonders for the moderns, were at Ephesus; and it is recorded that the personal accomplishments and taste of her citizens were celebrated throughout surrounding regions. All these she had (as many cities of modern Europe have still), and yet, having eyes, her citizens saw not the prevailing corruption; and having ears, they heard not the sentence of condemnation written against them.

What they needed, first of all, was light to discern the evil nature of sin; and second, that *personal sense of the evil* which would lead them to escape from it, and endeavor to rescue others. Until they saw their sin and felt its evil, they could make no advances in moral character.

Now, Paul affirmed in relation to these men, and to this subject two things—that whatever they saw to be evil in their former practice was made manifest to them by the moral light of the gospel, and that whatsoever makes sin manifest, as the gospel does, is light.

Once more. Notice that this state of intellectual culture and moral blindness was not confined to the old world. The same is true of the moderns. Our own country does not remind one of the union between culture and sin, as do the cities of Europe. Paris, with her academy, her columns, her galleries of painting, her statuary, her cathedrals, her philosophers, her oratories, her taste and fashion, her every thing that is deemed a mark of high intellectual culture—Paris, with all these, is the brothel of nations—a city where every species of moral corruption festers and infects the inhabitants, and spreads moral contagion over the continent.

I have stood in her galleries at Versailles and the Louvre, and felt in my soul that her models of art were a curse to the people. They are adapted to gild the memory of those who, being corrupt in heart and profligate in practice, are now suffering the hell that awaits selfish and impure minds. Their undraped statuary imparts the infection of the old world's guilt to the new. The pictures of the old masters, and from them down even to David, sanctify the deeds of devils under the name of kings and cardinals. Thus the popular mind is led to reverence despots and evil-doers. Their popular religion is as impure as the orgies of Ephesus, and their moral corruption as great as hers. In my opinion, while art might lose something, progress and morality would gain much, if the next outbreak in Paris should destroy all the public galleries in the city. What is true of Paris, is true likewise of all the great cities of the continent where the people are without the light of revelation. Culture and crime prevail together, to some extent, even in Protestant cities; but there is as much moral difference between the Protestant cities of Geneva and Aberdeen on the one hand, and Florence and Naples on the other, as there is between daylight and darkness.

Intellectual culture without Christian culture, is a painted harlot, who lives in moral night; and, decorated in the tinsel of art and letters, allures the weak and the wicked to hell. Were there no hope for mankind but that which art, letters, and intellectual culture produces, despotism and darkness would reign over the earth, and the hope of moral progress, of human freedom, and human happiness, might be abandoned forever. Men might be as cultivated as was Robespierre, and yet become as dark-minded and as desperate as he. They might be as polished externally as was Dr. Webster, while yet internally they might be as wicked. John Newton had the same mind and the same intellectual culture when engaged in the slave-trade, that he afterward possessed when his muse charmed and purified the hearts of all those who listened to him.

In many and striking forms Christ taught men the difference between intellectual and Christian culture. The one without the other is "the whited sepulcher"—"the hidden grave"—the darkness or "night" of the soul. The one pertains to man's moral nature—his affections and his conscience—the other to his intelligence. The one without the other engenders selfishness and hypocrisy; but intellectual culture, used and sanctified by a living conscience and pure affections, secures all human good to its possessor, and leads him to labor for the good of the world. When the intellect moves to the work of human elevation, the power which gives the impulse and secures permanency, is generated in the heart and conscience. Men with intellectual light alone may make advances without moral principles, as they have done often in France, South America, and elsewhere; but without moral principle, which gospel faith produces, permanent progress is impossible.

With these principles and discriminations in mind, I now proceed to show that all human progress, both ancient and modern, has its origin in the truth and power of revealed religion; and that without this the hope of reform is fallacious, and if progress were attained, it could not be permanent.

It is a historical fact which has not been sufficiently noticed, that human nature is always below revelation. This fact indicates the divine origin of revelation. Great discoveries are usually the product of preceding ages of thought. One mind develops the idea; but it is the fruitage of the age ripened in that mind. A pearl is found; but the location had been indicated by previous researches. But revealed religion is something different from this. It is separate from and superior to the thought of the age. It calls the wisdom of the world foolishness, and introduces a new stand-point and starting-point, around which it gathers what was valuable in the old, and destroys the remainder. Hence it will always be found true that a struggle is necessary to bring up the human mind and keep it up to the level of revealed religion, and that revealed religion produces that struggle. The human mind *naturally* falls below it; hence frequent struggles are necessary to restore it from its relapses. Even those who profess to be the friends of the dispensation, retrograde so soon as its power is in any wise abated; and new applications of the *same power* have to be made to rescue them, and bring them up again nearer to the requirements of their dispensation.

No one will doubt but that the theology of Moses was antagonistic to that of Egypt, and to that of all the nations with which the Israelites had intercourse. Its great aim was to destroy idolatry, to remove physical and moral impurities, and establish the worship of the one true God, Jehovah. But the Jews (although all their traditions were in favor of monotheism, and all their experiences such as were adapted to drive them from idolatry) were constantly falling into the vices and idolatries of surrounding nations. Their history is a record of sad departures from the purity of the Mosaic economy.

Now, the question is, by what means was the advanced system maintained and reformation produced, when the people had again dropped down to their natural level? We answer, by the power of revealed truth, and by this alone. "Whatsoever was reproved in Israel, was made manifest by the light," and "whatsoever does make manifest is light."

Their defections were shown to them by referring them to the light of the law of Moses. This alone could show them the evil of polytheism, for no other system existed in the world that did not favor the evil. The evil being revealed *by the law*, they were *reproved out of the same* law for departing from its requirements, and in this way alone reformations were produced. The instances of reformation by the light and power of the revealed religion I need not to enumerate, especially to you. The relapses were all recovered, and the nation finally delivered from all disposition to idolatry, by the Bible, and by the providence of God working in harmony with the dispensation—punishing departures and encouraging reform.

When the nation was almost lost in the surrounding darkness, the Reformation under Josiah was produced by the law alone. "The Book" found—as Luther found it afterwards in the convent—was the light and power of the rescue.

In the later periods of the dispensation, the old prophets stood up in the solemn grandeur of their mission, to *reprove* the rulers and the people, and restore them to obedience to the law. The voices of Jeremiah, of Isaiah and Ezekiel, are heard in tones of sorrow, instruction, and reproof, reverberating through the nation. They held aloft the law, and showed to the people that the judgments of God would come, or had come, upon them for departing from it. They gave the law a spiritual import in advance of what it had before [a characteristic of the true preacher]; they enforced it by the authority of God; and spoke almost with the tongue of an evangelist of a future Messiah. Thus, in the light of the law they reproved in the name of God: and if reformation was not produced, they led the people to feel that judgment came upon them for disobedience; and thus their captivities and sufferings tended finally to cure their errors.

Now, I need not say to you, what you know, that by this process, and this alone, was the worship of one God at length established in the world. By the law of Moses, and the administration of the reproving prophets, the thing was accomplished, and in no other way. Thus the law was a schoolmaster to bring us to Christ. When the evil of idolatry was cured, and ideas of the Messiah created by the Mosaic ritual, the world was prepared for a higher dispensation.

One other topic here is worthy of notice. It is a part of the history of monotheism that has not been sufficiently studied. I allude to the history of the Arabians, as it connects itself with the Old Testament on the one side, and with Islamism on the other. The Arabs claim Abraham, the first reformer of the world, as their father. Ishmael was the son of the father of the faithful; but his son by a foreign wife; yet to Ishmael also was the promise given, that he should inherit—but in an inferior degree—the blessing of Abraham. Other descendants of Abraham were mingled in Idumea, constituting two lines of the Abrahamic family—the Arabic and the Jewish. They have the same relation to the true religion that the two sons have to Abraham, or Esau and Jacob to Isaac. Through the true son comes the true gospel; the other is a degree removed from it. But the fact is, that both lines recognize and worship the same one God: from both originate the reformers of idolatry. The Arabs are now, in this respect, about where the Jews were before the coming of Christ. They, like the Jews, have frequently relapsed into the idolatry and vices of surrounding nations; yet before Mohammed there were many reformers who restored monotheism in some of the tribes. But the points at which this history connects itself with our subject are, first, the Mohammedans are monotheists; second, they worship Jehovah, the God of Abraham and Moses; third, mark it, *this reformation of the Arabian tribes, which restored the worship of the one*

God, was effected by Mohammed through the light and power of the patriarchal and Mosaic dispensations. The truth which the prophet uses to kill idolatry is drawn from the history of Abraham and the precepts of Moses. The 14th chapter of the Koran is entitled "Abraham." The patriarch is introduced as praying for the suppression of idolatry—"Keep me and my children from the worship of idols; they have seduced part of the people." The authority of Moses is likewise recognized, and he is frequently introduced as denouncing idolatry and commanding the worship of Jehovah.

Thus, the evidence is palpable and incontrovertible, that the worship of one God revealed in the Old Testament Scriptures, has been the reforming power of the whole world, so far as man is rescued from idolatry. The two branches of the Abrahamic family have done the work. Mohammedans are now, in this one respect, where the Jews were before Christ, and where the unbelieving Jews are still. All that they have in advance of heathen polytheism is by the revealed religion of the Old Testament, and the authority of Jehovah as there revealed. All that we have in advance of them starts from this point. This brings us to the gospel dispensation—the "*true light that now shineth.*"

The prophets of the old dispensation, as we have noticed, had foretold the sevenfold light of the Messianic age. The last prophetic utterance (Mal. iii. 1–4) announces that Christ would send his messenger (John Baptist) before him; that he would suddenly come in his temple; but that his dispensation would be "*as a refiner's fire*"—a moral power, purifying the world and the church.

John Baptist came, and affirming that the kingdom of heaven was at hand, he called the nation to repentance; thus practically promulgating the truth that reformation was necessary in order to enter the Messiah's kingdom. This was the burden of his baptism—"The axe is laid at the root of the tree." The separating fan is in the hand of the Messiah. He will separate the chaff from the wheat—gather the wheat into his garner, and burn the chaff with unquenchable fire.

Jesus came, preaching reformation and a higher life. He denounced the traditions of the Jewish teachers. He selected men without literary or philosophical attainment. He imbued them with a new spirit, and with power from on high; and commissioned them to revolutionise all forms of power in church and state; promising divine aid and supervision until the work should be accomplished.

You know the result. You know the struggle and the success of the truth in the apostolic age. As it was in Ephesus, so it was in other cities. When Jesus died, the old world had its greatest intellectual light, and its greatest moral darkness. The truth and power of the gospel was a purifying element, reforming and elevating out of the mass of corruption a large company of the men of that age.

In establishing a new system, with new powers and principles, the agency of the Divine Author must be interposed, of course; just as every new geological advance requires divine interposition. But as human nature is always below the revealed religion which is designed to reform and elevate it, the corrupt age, and the dark ages which followed, were a natural sequence. The last of the apostles was not in his grave, and the visible power which established the New Testament had scarcely subsided, before humanity lapsed into error. To the light of the apostolic age there succeeded clouds, darkened by depravity and tinged by superstition. When earthly power could not subdue the church, it allied itself with her, and thus corrupted her truth; and from the period of the adulterous union between church and state the light of truth waned into the total eclipse of the dark ages—ages without a Bible.

But out of the darkness a light sprung up which has shone more and more down to our day. Now, our last inquiry is, Has revealed religion been the source and the power of reformation and moral progress in the world, under the Christian dispensation, and from the dark ages until now?

We need not inquire concerning the causes which immediately introduced the dark ages. Suffice it to say, that during the period from the sixth to the fifteenth century, the light of revelation was vailed. The Scriptures were no longer in the vernacular tongue of the people. Both church and state were without a Bible. The dawn of reformation begins with Wicklif and Huss. Their translations and preaching ante-date the art of printing, and the other great inventions of the fifteenth century. The art of printing no doubt greatly aided the Reformation. But printing in itself has no reformatory *moral* power in it. Whether it advances or retards the civil and moral progress of men depends on the things printed. The enemies of the Reformation used the press as freely as the reformers. The press infected the continent with atheism in the days of Voltaire, and the press strengthened the power of despotism under Robespierre. The press can do no more than disseminate the thought of the age, whether that be bad or good. Truth is stronger than error; hence the press is an auxiliary in the world's enlightenment. But light without moral principle has no real reformatory power. It does not create conscience, and hence wants the element of permanent moral progress.

Luther is identified as *the man* of the Reformation. Whence did Luther draw his power? A benighted monk, he found a copy of the Bible in the convent of Erfurth. The Bible enlightened Luther. He translated it into the vernacular tongue of his country, and it enlightened the people. Every shaft that the reformers hurled at the Papal demon was drawn from the Bible. Nine tenths of the literature of the Reformation was biblical. That the Bible made the reformers is as true as that the reformers produced the Reformation *by the same means.* About the facts in the case there can be no controversy. The dark ages were dissipated, and the Reformation accomplished by the light and power of revealed religion.

You have, no doubt, read the recently-published history of the Dutch Republic, by Motley. If you have not, get it at once. It will give you the detailed statement of the struggle between the Bible power and the Papal devil in the Netherlands—a struggle, the successful issue of which placed Holland in the forefront of the civilization of the age, furnished an asylum for the persecuted in other nations, and developed a degree of moral progress greatly in advance of the times. That the Bible power achieved this moral victory for humanity, freedom and religion can not be questioned.

It is conceded that the basis for the Reformation in England was laid by Tindall's translation. Beside this, during the struggle in the Netherlands, multitudes of the persecuted fled to England, and carried the seeds of Bible truth with them across the Channel. Thus was begun the progress that was rendered permanent by the translation under King James.

Another stage of progress in civil and religious freedom was initiated by the Puritans. To them it is conceded, even by Macaulay, that England owes all that places her in advance of other Protestant nations of Europe. To them, and the Scotch and Dutch Puritans, we owe all of religious liberty that we possess in America. And yet who dare deny that all these stages of progress were gained by the Bible power? The questions of those ages of progress were Bible questions. The conscience that strengthened true moral heroes to endure and to triumph was Bible-made conscience. The issues between them and their opponents were Bible issues. Luther's moving issue was justification by faith against the error of justification by penance and indulgences. The Dutch and the Scotch fought against the powers of darkness, and triumphed under the same banner. The Puritans inscribed on their banner "Bible faith and practice against forms." The pure Bible was their watchword. Wesley's Reformation was purely religious, but, like preceding advances, it was founded on Bible principle—experience against profession. So the principle of Penn was non-conformity to the world, against a worldly church. But more than all, it was Bible faith which gave strength of *heart* and *conscience* and *will* to these reformers; so that they braved dangers, suffered persecutions, subdued the wilderness, and achieved all the civil and religious progress which the world possesses.

This historic analysis might be run through all the details of human progress. So far as the human families have advanced in moral culture, with its concomitant blessings of civil liberty and social comfort, that advance has been achieved—even in limited localities—by Bible light and power.

But this long letter must be closed. Take an epitome of instances and illustrations.

In my school-days we had a map in our geographies which gave us an apprehension of the degree of civilization existing in different countries of the globe. Those regions which were the most advanced in civil and moral culture, were light; the utterly pagan regions were black; those regions partially civilized were partially radiated. Now, upon that map, which I took pains to inquire for and examine very recently, the degree of national enlightenment corresponds precisely with the amount of Bible knowledge prevalent among the people. There is no exception to this. It is universal over the whole earth. The Bible is the light and life of the moral world, just as distinctly as the sun is the light and life of the physical world.

The local illustrations of this fact are striking. I have had the privilege, in various portions of the old and new world, of noticing evidences that have left lasting impressions on my heart. Allow me, in conclusion, to give you a transcript of these impressions.

Various states of Germany contain a mixed popution—some Protestant, some Papal inhabitants. Now, just in proportion to the Protestant element does moral progress and civil liberty exist. Take Belgium as the starting-point. Travel up the Rhine and through the German states toward Rome, and the amount of progress can be gaged accurately by the amount of Bible knowledge among the people. As you approach Rome, the seat of Papal power and superstition, the darkness can be felt. There the Bible is totally withheld from the masses, and the despotism of the rulers, and the degradation of the people, and the superstition of the whole, are almost equal to that of Central Asia; while vice and crime are more prevalent than they are in Central Africa.

Pass from Paris—at the same time the Athens and the Sodom of the continent—to Geneva, and thence to the Sardinian Alps.

Bible-reading Protestants preponderate in Switzerland; hence civil freedom prevails, and there is piety and probity among the peasantry, which contrasts favorably with the Catholic French. But in passing from Geneva, by Lake Leman to Chamouni, you pass from the Protestant canton Vaud into the Catholic canton Valais. Here moral night follows day without an intervening twilight. The dress, the physiognomy, the habits of the people change at once. In one you meet no beggars. In the other the road is thronged with them. In both, the peasants are poor; but in one there are evidences of honest industry, and you meet open, frank countenances; in the other poverty, with uncouth garments and sinister aspect. The more broken character of the country may have something to do with this; but the Bible power makes a difference that can be felt by the traveler.

Pass with me, now, through Scotland and Ireland. Scotland has one curse in common with Ireland—the habit of using ardent spirits prevalent among all classes. But apart from this, the peasantry are equal to any in Europe. In the cities of Edinburg and Glasgow there is a degree of poverty and vice in some of the poorer streets (as in High and Cowgate streets, Edinburg) which is revolting. I saw nothing like it in Aberdeen. On inquiring of an intelligent gentleman the reasons of the phenomenon, he said most of the mass of depravity accumulated in these pens was made up of Irish Catholics and similar elements; and that scarcely any of it originated with the Bible-reading population of the country.

Pass from Glasgow to Belfast, in Ireland; and from Belfast through Dublin to the south of the island. In this journey, as you leave the Bible-reading north, and pass to the Catholic south, you pass from light and morals into the heart of one of the most degraded and superstitious regions that there is in Europe. Perhaps, after the masses of Rome and Naples, there is none more so in Christendom.

Now, sir, look with me, a moment, over the different sections of our own country. You will agree with me that the most intelligent and moral population of the world, take them *en masse*, is in that portion of the Union where the people are most generally instructed in the Bible principle and precept; while in other sections of our land vice and ignorance prevail just in proportion as the people are deprived of the Bible; or in proportion as they suppress Bible truth in professedly Christian churches. In the one section principles and practices are maintained that would have appalled the men of the same section twenty years ago. In the other, I hope the light is advancing.

It is likewise true that all the moral reforms for which our land is distinguished, so far as they have succeeded, have been initiated and advanced by the Bible light and power in the hearts and consciences of reformers. The temperance movement began in the church; and the process of enlightenment was carried forward almost exclusively by Christians. Search the record, and you will find that the impulse and the direction were both given by Bible readers. I know the final appeal has been to legislation ; but legislation can do nothing until sufficient light is disseminated and sufficient conscience produced in relation to the evil to be reformed. Our legislation, in some States, has gone in advance of the moral sentiment of the masses, and reaction has ensued ; and the reform will never become prevalent until the light and moral power of the Bible produce sufficient-conscience to sustain it. There only is the moral principle that creates perseverance —there the benevolence that prompts to *persistent self-denial for human good.*

So in relation to the anti-slavery reform. In England, the Christian sentiment of the nation began, carried forward, and consummated the work of emancipation. In this country, the first fifteen years were spent entirely in moral endeavor by Bible men. It is true that a large portion of the churches withheld their influence, especially those churches rendered conservative by wealth, or connection with the sin ; but after all, it is true that in every region of the free States where the reform was urged perseveringly, and one advance after another secured, in every such instance, it will be found that the Bible power was the impulse, and Christians the agents in the work. There are parties who claim to be anti-slavery men, *par excellence*, of whom this can not be said; but these are self-elated and impracticable parties, united by idiosyncrasies, and utterly infeasible in their aims, as they are uncharitable in their spirit.

But, enough. I appeal to you, my dear sir, whether the idea that human progress can be achieved without the Bible be not a fallacy, branded as such both by the principles developed in the preceding letter, and by the historical statements and illustrations of the present one? My logic, as you were pleased to call it, is verified by the facts of history. Revealed religion is the Alpha and the Omega of human progress.

Yours, my dear sir, for that light which makes evil manifest, reproves it when made manifest, and thus abates it in the world.

J. B. W.

APPENDIX.

EXTRACT FROM THE NEW ENGLANDER OF MAY, 1856.

Our previous article* refers the whole question of man's immortality to the will of God. An argument from nature is only our inference of that will from the disclosures of God in the material universe and in the consciousness of the human soul. In these, and especially in the latter, we find evidence of a God of wisdom, justice, and goodness. From these attributes the inference is irresistible, to a divine will, ordaining endless existence to all to whom such an existence would be an endless progress in virtue and bliss. But in regard to those irrevocably moving toward an opposite moral destiny, the voice of nature, though unmistakably predicting a *future life* as a necessity of divine justice and moral government, seems to some not so explicitly to assure immortality. Contrawise, rather, the very attributes of the Godhead, which guaranty to the good an everlasting being, might be regarded as necessarily dooming the wicked to ultimate annihilation; or at least as creating, in behalf of that doctrine, so strong a presumption as to be entitled materially to modify and control our interpretation of the Scriptures.

Our argument thus far has been engaged in combating such a presumption; in showing the insufficiency of the grounds and the invalidity of the assumptions on which it rests; and that

---

* New Englander, Feb., 1856.

our ignorance of the moral system and economy under which we now are, ill entitles us to dogmatize in regard to that which is to be. The very same difficulties and mysteries embarrass the existence of evil in the present world that are supposed to forbid its existence in the eternal future,* and they require, as far as we can see, that the wicked should never have been at all, not less than that they should forever cease to be. Our ignorance of the law or principle which underlies the origin and continuance of evil, makes us incompetent to limit its scope and duration. But reasoning from the analogy of nature, we should infer from its existence, spite of seeming mysteries and difficulties, its not improbable co-existence with them hereafter.

Still there are minds in our times—minds, too, which we respect for sagacity, erudition, and piety—that do take this term of doom in another sense. We raise no question of their candor or sincerity, but we can not resist the impression that with them, though without their consciousness, natural theology is father to revealed; and that philosophy and prejudgment of what the word of God *must* teach, have much to do with their interpreting what it *does* teach. They contend that everlasting punishment means, or at least is compatible with, annihilation. They maintain that *everlasting punishment*, even if everlasting be taken in the sense of endless, which they affirm can be questioned, does not of necessity imply *everlasting existence;* that its import may be satisfied by a punishment whose *effects* are everlasting, i. e., one from which there shall be no recovery.

They claim, moreover, that such a limitation of the term is necessary to reconcile it with other Scripture, where words significant of utter and total extinction of being are applied to the future destiny of the wicked, such as *death*, *destruction*, "*everlasting destruction*," *perishing*, *perdition*, and the like. They

* This is at least a doubtful statement. The past is, in all the series below man, a progressive system—the higher types being advanced, while those unfitted for new and better conditions are not restored but destroyed.

tell us, moreover, that Jesus Christ is presented in the Scriptures as the author of life; and that eternal life—by which they understand eternal existence—is promised by him to those only who believe in him; while death, or the negation of existence, is denounced as the doom of those who believe not; and, moreover, that the agent or instrument of future punishment, "*fire*," is one whose nature is to consume, not conserve in pain, so that, whether it is to be interpreted figuratively or literally, it is evidently designed to convey the idea of the utter destruction of its victim. Such are the grounds, philological and exegetical, upon which the argument for annihilation is defended, and on which, presumptions from nature being abandoned, it must be sustained, if at all.

Now the simple question before us, we premise here, is, What is a fair interpretation of language? Not, what is suitable to our notions of God's nature or government; or what may arm the gospel with the most powerful incentives; or what may seem to us most safe or expedient to promulgate; or what most enhances the value of the soul. Such considerations we discard as alien to our present inquiry, and tending only to perturb the mind with influences having no connection with evidences of truth or falsehood. It is not ours, in determining a question of divine doctrine, to inquire after what is safe or prudent to be taught, or what is requisite to give motive power to the gospel, or dignity to the human soul. These questions are God's; and we best seek their solution when we inquire, what is truth? what is God's teaching and God's arrangement? Let us not presume to be wiser than God, or to understand better than he the true forces of the gospel. Nor, again, let us permit the logical and philological import of language to be overruled by our fears for God's honor, or the integrity of his wisdom, justice, and benevolence. God will care for his own honor, and he knows perfectly what is congruous with his wisdom, justice, and goodness. *God* hath spoken! we have to do, simply, with the inquiry, What hath he said? God hath spoken *to man*. He has spoken, then, according to the laws of human language, and is to be interpreted according to the laws of human speech. The question before us now, let us bear in mind, then, is not one of philosophy, but purely of criticism, philologic and exegetical. It bears through awful deeps, it is true, but they are deeps beyond our *philosophic* soundings; and there is the more need, manifestly, that we follow, in childlike trust and simplicity, the divine voice.

Our present argument claims, that approached and interpreted in this spirit, the Scriptures do teach the immortal existence of the wicked, by direct, deliberate, formal declarations, as well as by implication, in numerous passages; and that the words and phrases alleged to convey a contrary doctrine, are, when applied to the soul, not only susceptible of a limitation and modification of import which may avoid such contradiction, but are actually employed in the familiar and constant usage of the Scriptures, in such application, with such limitation and modification of meaning. It claims, moreover, that those terms which, applied to the body, denote dissolution and destruction, find, when predicated of the soul, their analogy most perfectly met, and have an especial appositeness of significancy in indicating spiritual ruin; that they are actually in common use in the Scriptures, without denoting extinction of being, but with the unquestionable significancy of a spiritual corruption; and that the mind at once recognizes the fitness of the usage, and feels that the import of the terms is satisfied, and the analogy of signification, required in the application to the soul, is fully met in such usage. They can, therefore, thus interpreted, be reconciled with the direct, obvious import of the passages declarative of the future doom of the wicked, without doing any violence to language; whereas the contrary process—controlling the direct, explicit, and declarative, by the indirect, the allusive, incidental, and inferential—violates a common canon of interpretation.

RULING TEXTS.

Let us now examine some of those passages of Scripture that may seem entitled to be regarded as *ruling texts* on this question; that is, those that with the most deliberateness, distinctness, and solemn formality, set forth the process of final judgment; or with the most fullness and explicitness characterize the future doom of the lost. And first, perhaps, among these, the judgment scene in the 25th chapter of Matthew, demands our attention, as entitled, because of its calm, deliberate, didactic character, and its freedom from the excitements and coloring of imagination or passion, as well as its greater explicitness and fullness, to rank among the leading passages—the "*loci classici*" of Scripture—on the theme of human destiny. The imagery employed is purely for the purpose of instruction and elucidation, not rhetorical or emotive. The spirit pervading it coheres with the time and scene. It is a case where he, who is himself to be the future Judge, sitting on the brow of Olivet, in secluded and calm converse with the disciples, who are waiting to receive from his lips the word, that they may proclaim it through ages, sets forth the process and sentence of the last judgment, and the separate destinies of the two great moral divisions of our race. The shadows of the hastening crucifixion are falling around the speaker. Life is entering the solemnity of its last hour. The theme, the speaker, the time, the scene—all are above poetry, above passion; too awful for rhetoric; all belong to severe reason and pure truth. Word and phrase now mean all they utter. No abatement is required for amplification or embellishment, for enthusiasm or fanaticism. Terrible as they are, still we must regard them as dispassionate and severely true, even as the doom they utter, belonging, if ever did words uttered in this world, to the intensely, utterly, eternally real. Let us so interpret them. They present before us the judgment scene as connecting, in the divine government, two eternities;

and with its double aspect toward the everlasting. The Son of man has come in his glory; before him are gathered all nations; the division is made, and sentence and execution thus proceed. "Then shall the King say to those on his right hand, Come, ye blessed of my Father! inherit the kingdom prepared for you before the foundation of the world." * * * "And then shall the King say also to those on the left hand, Depart, ye cursed, into everlasting fire, prepared for the devil and his angels."* "And these shall go away into everlasting punishment, and the righteous into life eternal"†—or everlasting; the epithet in the original is the same as that just applied to the punishment.

Such is Jesus Christ's statement of the final destiny of man. It is *final;* there is nothing beyond—no reappearance or re-adjudication. From that judgment scene they pass to return no more. They disappear in the unapproachable light, or the impenetrable darkness. One would at first suppose the words of Christ in this case were so explicit and positive in assertion of the immortality of man—good or evil—that they could not be made more so; that the hermeneutics that could evade them would defy any grasp of human language. But still, as their import has been questioned, let us aim to develop it in formal propositions. Now, no one will dispute that a text asserts the immortality of the wicked, if the three following propositions can be established in regard to it:

1st. *It describes the doom of the wicked after death.*

2d. *It predicates of that doom eternal duration.*

3d. *That doom implies the continued existence of its subject.*

Let us apply these propositions to the above passage:

First, THE PASSAGE RELATES TO THE DOOM OF THE WICKED AFTER DEATH. This is unquestionable. The scene is the last judgment; the sentence, the final reward; the history, the last disclosed in the empire of God.

---

* Matt., xxv., 34–41. † Ibid, 46.

Second, THE DOOM AFFIRMED OF THEM IS OF ETERNAL DURATION. The adjective of time used asserts this; it is the one that would naturally have been employed to express that idea. It answers in import and usage to its English representative *eternal* and *everlasting*. By its probable etymology (*αἰώνιος αἰών, ἀεί,*) it denotes the ALWAYS-BEING, or EVER-BEING; its radix being the adverb of perpetuity, or continuance. In actual usage, it regularly carries, in all its modifications, the sense of time *unlimited if not illimitable.* It is the proper adjective of eternity, so much so, that in common usage of the Scriptures it is applied characteristically to God, signifying his eternity.* The original Greek had no stronger epithet of duration. It is true that, like its English representatives, it is sometimes attached to objects of a measurable date. But such usage belongs to rhetorical and poetic diction, or to the language of imagination and passion, or appears with obvious limitations in the nature or relations of the subject to which it attaches; (as, e. g., everlasting hills; everlasting statutes, etc.). Such cases, however, indicate and explain themselves. Apart from such diction and limitation, expressed or implied, the term, of its own proper force, carries the idea of eternal duration. But in this text is no such diction; nor is there any such limitation, unless in the nature of the soul, to suppose which, begs the entire question by assuming the very point at issue, or in some popular notion of the soul's mortality, prevalent at the time—but such notions did not prevail among those to whom Christ spake.

For again, amid the strongest proofs that Christ here designed by the term "everlasting" to convey the idea of endless duration, is the historic fact that the Jews, with their ideas of the immortality of the soul, must have so understood it. The Jews in Christ's time—all who believed the soul would exist at all after death—believed it would never die. For this fact Josephus expressly and explicitly testifies: "The doctrine of the

---

* Rom. xvi. 22. Sept. Gen. xxi. 33. Isa. xl. 28, etc.

Essenes is this: That bodies are corruptible, and the matter they are made of, not permanent; but that souls are immortal and continue forever. * * * And indeed the Greeks seem to me to have followed the same notion, when they allot the islands of the Blessed to their brave men, and to the souls of the wicked, the region of the ungodly in Hades; where such persons as Sisyphus, Tantalus, and Ixion, and Tityus are punished; which is built on this first supposition that souls are immortal; whereby bad men are restrained by the fear and expectation they are in, that although they should lie concealed in this life, they should suffer IMMORTAL PUNISHMENT AFTER DEATH."

Of the Pharisees, Josephus also testifies, "they say that all souls are incorruptible, but that the souls of bad men are subject to ETERNAL PUNISHMENT." But the Sadducees take away the belief of the immortal duration of the soul, and the punishments and rewards in Hades.*

Again, elsewhere, he testifies, "The Pharisees believe that souls have an immortal vigor in them; that under the earth there will be rewards or punishments according as they have lived virtuously or viciously in this life; the latter are to be detained in an EVERLASTING PRISON, but that the former shall have power to revive and live again. * * * But the doctrine of the Sadducees is that souls die with the bodies."†

Such is the testimony of the Jewish historian cotemporary with Christ. The sects embracing the doctrine of immortality were the great majority of the nation; those rejecting it, rejected a future life altogether. Our Saviour, therefore, in that discourse, must have been understood by those who heard him, as meaning, by the term in question, strictly *everlasting;* and he knew he must be so understood. Of course, using it without limitations, he designed to be so understood; and such must be its meaning in the passage.

---

* Josephus' Wars of the Jews: Book II. Chap. viii. Sects. 11–14.

† Antiquities of the Jews: Book XVIII. Chap. i. Sects. 3–4.

That then it should have here its proper import of ever-during, would seem plainly inferrible from the *nature of the subject*, from the *time and scope of the scene* described, from the *notions prevalent on the theme of discourse* amid those to whom the description was addressed, and from the *definition of the term in the context*, in application to a subject—the life of the righteous—to which none think of applying a restricted signification. Instead, then, of the word everlasting being here restricted in its natural signification, it appears to us expanded by the character of its subject, and by the occasion and the auditory, to its infinite capacity.

As predicated of the *soul* and especially the *doom of the soul after the last judgment*, we may say without begging the question, the terms everlasting and eternal, to the common mind and usage, carry the idea of endless duration. For however imperfect and unsettled may be the notions of men in regard to the immortality of the soul, they do not think of using or understanding the terms, eternal and everlasting, in relation to it or its future destiny, in a limited import. The mind naturally, if admitting the existence of the spirit after death at all, conceives of it as among the most enduring of things. Especially would a limited import be attached to an epithet describing the *final doom* of the soul, because that doom is the very uttermost syllable of its history. It covers the infinite future. Bearing this, the soul disappears from view forever. No ulterior judgment, no reversal of doom is intimated. Every aspect of the scene and transaction looks to the everlasting. The personages with differences of moral character and history, are dismissed from that throne on destinies that shall turn back no more. If the scope of any scene or action could sustain in common usage the unlimited extent of the time-term employed, surely this were such an one. If that doom were not to cover the unlimited future, and that life and punishment were to be consummated, and have an end, we should expect, in a professed exhibit of man's destiny, some intimation of it.

Moreover, our Lord obviously would not have used, in such a case, language which he knew would have been misapprehended, with no explanation or caution, or any intimation at all guarding against misconstruction. And certainly he would not have done so, knowing as he must, that by the use of the same word in the next clause, where none would think of limiting it, viz., in application to the happy destiny of the righteous, he would necessarily be understood by hearers and readers as fixing its meaning. According to all rules of fair and perspicuous speech, the term which applied to the life of the righteous in one clause embraces endless being, can not in one immediately adjacent shrink into finite and measurable date.

Thirdly. THIS DOOM IMPLIES CONTINUANCE OF BEING IN ITS OBJECTS. The words everlasting *punishment* imply this. This might seem too obvious and self-evident for argument. But some contend that these words may import simply a punishment everlasting in its consequences (one from which there shall never be a recovery), and may thus be fully satisfied by the annihilation of those punished. But that these words have not this meaning here, is clear from the following considerations. *This is not the natural and obvious import of the words;* that import by which, according to the laws of sound criticism, we ought to interpret language, in the circumstances in which this was uttered, and according to which the phrase was unquestionably understood by those who heard it. We think we certainly are not mistaken in feeling that "everlasting punishment" is not the term in which one would naturally have expressed the idea of the extinction of being; some other word than "punishment" would have been used. Again, *that is not the proper meaning of the phrase employed.* The word translated punishment, κόλασις, is a word denoting, not the consequence, but the act of punishing. It is a verbal noun, *a nomen actionis,* equivalent not to an *opus operatum* (a work operated), but to the operation. It indicates not result so much as process. It is stronger than the common word rendered punishment, the word employed with its adjective by Josephus to indicate eternal or immortal punishment (τιμωρία). It is more significant than atonement, amercement, expiation, penal satisfaction, etc. It corresponds more nearly to our word *chastisement*, and might not inaptly have been rendered *punishing* instead of punishment. It is a noun of infliction. Its prime etymological idea is that of maiming, cutting, mutilation, and the like. In common usage it implies conscious suffering in its object. It is the same word which is rendered torment in 1 John, iv. 18; where it is said, "There is no fear in love, because fear hath *torment.*" This is the only other passage exhibiting this word in the New Testament. If translated in this manner in the clause under inspection, ambiguity of meaning would have been impossible. We regard the word, therefore, as implying its proper force, and because of the popular belief amid those to whom the word was addressed, the conscious existence of its subject. Again, we infer this doom carries the idea of conscious being, *because of the adjunct attached to the instrument of the punishment predicated* (whether in reality or figure is immaterial). That instrument or adjunct is called *everlasting fire.* But why apply the epithet everlasting to the agent, unless to convey the idea of everlasting action? and what pertinency in calling the action everlasting, if the suffering were not to be so? It certainly would seem frivolous to say the fire was everlasting, but the torment inflicted was not so. The only pertinency in the use of this adjective of endless duration attached to the penal agent, is found in the implication of correspondent duration of the suffering of those subjected to its power. The sentencing to a fire which shall burn forevermore, would be naturally understood to be a sentencing to burn in it forevermore. The adjunct were nugatory otherwise. So of everlasting fire here; it were childish to accumulate epithets upon the fire for any other end. Would God attempt to create terror by a mere sonorous and idle play of words? Would our Saviour—would the great Judge—resort to a mere trick of language, a childish illusion of the imagination?

What matters it to souls absolutely and forever to be burned up, whether the fire that consumes them should raven on through eternal ages, or is to be quenched with the extinction of their own being? whether they are consumed in a bonfire or in the conflagration of worlds? If I am to be drowned, what matters it whether it be in the rivulet or the Atlantic? It surely were unworthy of the awful dignity and truthfulness of the scene, for the Judge in his sentence before the assembled universe, thus to dilate on the everlastingness of the fire, when he knew the culprits sentenced would soon be forever beyond its burning. Let it burn on forever, it could not reach them. What would its endless rage, even should it devour the universe, be to them in the bosom of eternal nothing? Certainly the sentence of the last day will not attempt to frighten the condemned by a childish play on unreal fears. If the application of the epithet everlasting, to the fire, does not import that the lost ones punished by it are to be everlastingly exposed to its fury, it would be hard to acquit the final sentence of falsifying the obvious, designed, and inevitable impression of language, by a mere artful equivoque worthy of a Pagan oracle. But the scene and the speaker drive such a thought wide as the universe aloof.

Suppose the sentence had been, Depart, ye cursed, into fire that shall burn a hundred years, or a thousand years, who would think otherwise than that those sentenced were to burn in that fire one hundred or one thousand years? We should all think of nothing else than taking an attributive of duration attached to the agent of punishment, as an assignment of the date to the punishment itself. We could discern no reason for its introduction at all if not for this purpose. So in case of the sentence of the great day, if the time-term of the fire is not meant to be that of its infliction of pain, we can see no reason why it is introduced here. Surely the eternal judgment were no theme nor scene for admitting an artful fetch, by indirection conveying a fallacy it shrinks from directly uttering. And surely he from whose lips these words fell—who was himself truth and love, and in whose mouth guile was never found—would not abuse and afflict men with unreal terrors; and especially by terrors which, as is contended, while afflicting man, only dishonor God. So subsequently in applying the epithet *everlasting* alike to the life of the righteous and the punishment of the wicked, in continuous clauses, we can not suppose our Lord, in pronouncing the irreversible doom, would palter in a double sense of the same word, making the life endless, but the penal suffering not so. Is everlasting punishment, in the common sense and usage of words, *simply punishment irreversible?*—punishment from which there shall be no recovery, irrespective of continuance of being? Does it not imply something *felt* everlastingly? Does an infliction merely extinctive of existence correspond to its common idea? Should we think of saying of a man shot or beheaded, that he departs into everlasting punishment, even though there is no recovery from it, and its effects are enduring? Is this a common-sense acceptation of the phrase? Would not the common mind understand more, and must it not have understood more by this when Christ uttered it? A punishment which the victim should forever suffer and from which he should find no rescue, nor release, nor reprieve? Punishment continuing implies existence continuing; everlasting punishment, everlasting existence. In common parlance you would no more speak of the punishment of the annihilated than of the uncreated.

Again, the words "everlasting punishment" imply everlasting continuance of being, because our Saviour must have *been conscious they conveyed that signification to those listening to him*, and his use of them, knowing they would be thus understood, makes him responsible for intending that signification. The Jews, with the notions entertained among them of the future destiny of the soul, could have interpreted them in no other way. The theory of extinction after judgment, had no place among them; the penal sufferings of the wicked, if there were any at all hereafter, were without end. But it is an established canon of interpretation, which construes the words of a fair and truthful speaker in the meaning in which he is conscious, while uttering them, they will be understood by the hearer. And evidently the Jewish mind, hearing words in customary use to indicate a common belief, with no indications of departure from that usage, could only understand by eternal punishment an immortal woe. This Jesus knew, and this he must have intended.

We think, then, our three propositions are proven in case of this text. It relates to the future doom of the wicked, affirms of that doom, eternity, and implies the continued conscious existence of its objects, viz., wicked souls.

This is the most full, formal, and methodic statement of the process and sentence of the final judgment to be found in the Scriptures, and taken in all its aspects, may be regarded as not less, certainly, than any other, a text entitled to rule on this topic. We pause here to inquire, then, whether the above passage, to one looking at it by itself, and bringing to its examination no theory to be established, and no prejudgments to be sustained, would not seem perfectly decisive of the whole question; so plain and so unambiguous, indeed, that there could be no mistaking its intent? DR. POST.

THE END.